MACHIAVELLI IN CHRISTENDOM

MACHIAVELLI IN CHRISTENDOM

Political Philosophy, Christianity, and Institutional Power

Don V. Pascal

MACHIAVELLI IN CHRISTENDOM: Political Philosophy, Christianity, and Institutional Power

First published 2026

Published by Demeter Academy Press, Los Angeles

ISBN: 978-1-971093-05-5 (print)

Printed in the United States of America

10 9 8 7 6 5 4 3 2 1

For those who entered institutions with open eyes

and stayed anyway

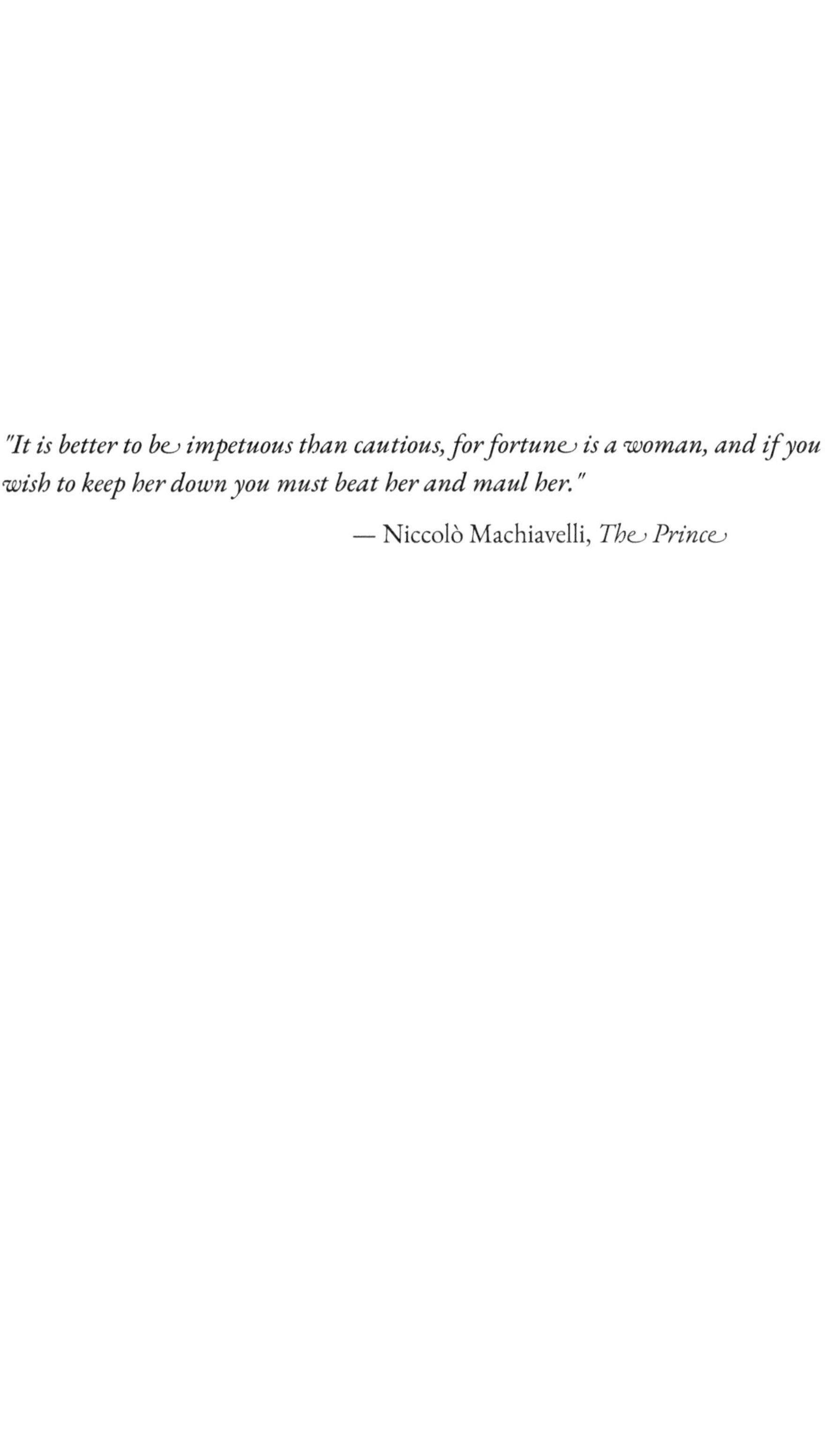

"It is better to be impetuous than cautious, for fortune is a woman, and if you wish to keep her down you must beat her and maul her."

— Niccolò Machiavelli, *The Prince*

Acknowledgments

This book was written in the space between institutions — a space that turns out to be more crowded than it appears.

I owe debts to teachers who taught me to read slowly, to colleagues who argued with me in good faith, and to the students who asked the questions I had been avoiding. Several of them will recognize their objections in these pages, rephrased as my own insights. I hope they will accept the theft as the compliment it is.

The scholars whose work made this book possible are named in the footnotes and bibliography, but a few require acknowledgment beyond citation. The framework of institutional analysis that runs through these pages draws on traditions of thought developed by Harold Berman, Ernst Kantorowicz, Charles Taylor, and Max Weber, among others. Where I have extended their arguments, the credit belongs to them; where I have distorted them, the fault is mine.

I am grateful to friends who read drafts at various stages and told me what they actually thought, which was not always what I wanted to hear. The book is better for their candor and shorter for their impatience.

Any errors of fact, interpretation, or judgment that remain are entirely my own.

Table of Contents

From Christendom to Now

INTRODUCTION

The Man Who Named the Machine

And many have imagined republics and principalities that have never been seen or known to exist in reality.

— Niccolò Machiavelli, The Prince

On the morning of May 6, 1527, an army crossed the Tiber and entered Rome.

The force that poured through the city's defenses was enormous, underpaid, and beyond the control of its commanders. It had been marching for weeks through central Italy under orders that no longer meant anything, fighting for wages that had not arrived. What held it together was momentum and hunger. When the walls of Rome gave way, the army did not occupy the city. It consumed it.

For eight days—and then for weeks beyond—soldiers moved through the streets of the capital of Western Christendom killing, looting, and burning. Churches were stripped. Archives were destroyed. Cardinals were ransomed in the streets. The pope, Clement VII, fled through a fortified corridor to the Castel Sant'Angelo and watched from its ramparts as the city he governed was taken apart below him.[1]

The army was technically commanded by Charles V, Holy Roman Emperor—the most powerful Christian ruler in the world, the man whose title encoded the idea that European civilization was a unified Christian order. Charles had not ordered the sack. He had simply failed to pay his troops and failed to control them, and the consequences followed as they always do when the gap between authority and capacity becomes impossible to sustain.[2]

When the news reached Florence, Niccolò Machiavelli was fifty-eight years old and had spent the last fifteen years in enforced retirement, stripped of the government position that had been the center of his adult life.[3] He had used those

[1] André Chastel, *The Sack of Rome*, 1527, trans. Beth Archer (Princeton: Princeton University Press, 1983), 160-170.
[2] Chastel, *Sack of Rome*, 199–210; Mallett and Shaw, *Italian Wars*, chap. 10.
[3] Maurizio Viroli, *Machiavelli* (Oxford: Oxford University Press, 1998), pp. 91–99.

years to write—about how states are founded and destroyed, about why Italian armies kept losing to foreign invaders, about the distance between the Christian principles that rulers proclaimed and the political mechanics that actually determined whether they survived. He died in June 1527, within weeks of the news from Rome. Whether he heard the full details is uncertain. That he would have recognized exactly what had happened is not.[4]

What failed in 1527 was not belief. The men who carried out the sack were Christians. Charles V spent years afterward expressing his horror at what had occurred and his devotion to the Church.

What failed was something more specific and more structural: the set of institutional arrangements that were supposed to translate belief into functioning political order. Clear lines of command. Reliable payment of soldiers. A papacy capable of maintaining political relationships alongside spiritual authority. The moral consensus was real. The institutional capacity was not, and when the two came apart, it was the capacity that mattered.

Machiavelli had spent his career watching exactly this kind of failure. He had watched it in the Italian city-states that hired mercenary armies instead of training their own citizens to fight, in Florence's republican institutions that generated elaborate constitutional procedures while remaining unable to defend themselves against the first serious military threat, in a papacy that wielded enormous moral authority while repeatedly undermining its own political position through short-term dynastic maneuvering.[5]

The pattern was always the same: institutions relying on moral language to do work that only structural capacity could actually do.

He named this mechanism with a phrase that has not improved with translation: *the effectual truth*. What matters in political life is not what rulers claim, not what institutions announce themselves to be, not the moral vocabulary

[4] Viroli, *Machiavelli*, pp. 237–244.

[5] Quentin Skinner, *Machiavelli: A Very Short Introduction* (Oxford: Oxford University Press, 2000), 7–14; Machiavelli, *The Prince*, trans. Harvey C. Mansfield (Chicago: University of Chicago Press, 1998), ch. 12.

in which authority is dressed.[6] What matters is what actually happens when authority is tested—whether enforcement holds, whether allies commit, whether the institutions that produce obedience in ordinary times can sustain it in crisis. The effectual truth is what you find when you strip away the performance and look at what endures.

This book is about that mechanism. It is also about the world in which Machiavelli discovered it—and without which he could not have discovered it at all.

The Book That Didn't Exist

I wrote this book because I went looking for it and it wasn't there.

I wanted a book that took Machiavelli seriously as a political analyst and took Christendom seriously as the civilization he was analyzing. Not a philosophy seminar on republicanism. Not a self-help manual for the ambitious. A book that examined the actual political infrastructure of medieval and Renaissance Christendom—its jurisdictions, its enforcement mechanisms, its internal contradictions—and used Machiavelli's framework to make sense of how it worked and why it broke down. That book did not exist, so I researched the one I wanted to read.

The scholarship on Machiavelli tends to split along a line that leaves the most interesting territory unexplored. On one side, you get the intellectual historians—careful, serious, and focused on Machiavelli as a philosopher of civic republicanism who recovered classical antiquity as an alternative to the Christian political inheritance. On the other side, you get the popular market, where Machiavelli has been turned into something like a Renaissance Patrick Bateman: a tactical genius for sociopaths, all manipulation and power moves, stripped of any historical context whatsoever.

The academic reading strips out the institutional grit. The popular reading strips out the intellect. Neither version bothers with the political civilization he was actually describing.

---

[6] Machiavelli, Niccolò, *The Prince*. Translated by Harvey C. Mansfield. Chicago: University of Chicago Press, 1998, ch. 15.

The gap has made Machiavelli the most misread political thinker in the Western tradition. His name functions as a label—shorthand for cynicism, manipulation, the idea that politics is simply power dressed in whatever clothes serve the moment. That reduction tells us almost nothing about what he actually wrote and a great deal about our discomfort with what he saw.

A Claim That Cuts Both Ways

The misreading has a specific source. We have been reading Machiavelli outside the world that made him. We treat him as a thinker who transcended his historical moment—a secular prophet of political realism whose insights float free of the fifteenth-century Florentine context that produced them. Some of the most influential scholarship reads him as a secular recovery of classical republican thought, a break from Christian political theology, a philosopher who turned his back on the civilization he inhabited to recover something older and cleaner.[7] On that reading, to understand Machiavelli you need to know your Livy and your Cicero. Christendom is the backdrop he was working against.

This book argues the opposite. You cannot understand Machiavelli without Christendom. And you cannot understand Christendom—as a political civilization, as a system of governance, as the institutional world that shaped European life for a thousand years—without Machiavelli.

Machiavelli's mind was formed by Christian institutions. He was educated in schools whose curriculum was Christian in content and form. He learned to write in Latin shaped by a millennium of Christian use. He worked in a chancery whose rhetorical traditions descended from monastic letter-writing practice.[8] His audience was Christian. His problems—faction, mercenaries, papal politics, the gap between moral aspiration and political survival—were the specific problems of a Christian civilization. He was not outside Christendom diagnosing it from

---

[7] Quentin Skinner, *The Foundations of Modern Political Thought*, vol. 1 (Cambridge: Cambridge University Press, 1978), 113–186; J.G.A. Pocock, *The Machiavellian Moment* (Princeton: Princeton University Press, 1975), 49–80; Leo Strauss, *Thoughts on Machiavelli* (Glencoe, IL: Free Press, 1958), 9–14.

[8] Paul F. Grendler, *Schooling in Renaissance Italy: Literacy and Learning, 1300–1600* (Baltimore: Johns Hopkins University Press, 1989), 142–161; Robert Black, *Humanism and Education in Medieval and Renaissance Italy* (Cambridge: Cambridge University Press, 2001), chaps. 1–3.

some neutral vantage point. He was deep inside it, and the intimacy is what made his analysis so precise and so uncomfortable.

The reverse is equally true. Christendom is not best understood through theology alone. For most of the people who lived inside it most of the time, it was primarily a political civilization: a system of overlapping jurisdictions, competing authorities, moral languages deployed in the service of institutional power, and enforcement mechanisms dressed in the vocabulary of divine sanction.[9] Understanding how it actually functioned—why it was stable in some periods and catastrophically fragile in others, why the same moral vocabulary could legitimate opposing claimants in the same conflict—requires exactly the kind of analytic attention Machiavelli provides.

What the Standard Readings Miss

There is a well-established tradition of reading Machiavelli as a thinker who recovered classical antiquity as an alternative to Christian political thought — who found in Rome and Greece a set of civic republican values that offered something fundamentally different from the medieval Christian inheritance.[10]

A classical-recovery reading of Machiavelli has a historical problem. The texts Machiavelli loved did not arrive to him from antiquity. They arrived through a thousand years of Christian transmission. The manuscripts he read had been copied by monks, annotated by clerical scholars, preserved in cathedral libraries, and interpreted through a framework that understood Roman history as providential—as part of the story God was telling through human events.[11] The humanist movement that shaped his intellectual formation was not a secular alternative to Christian culture. It was a development within it, conducted by men formed in Christian institutions, funded by Christian patrons, and carried

[9] Harold J. Berman, *Law and Revolution: The Formation of the Western Legal Tradition* (Cambridge, MA: Harvard University Press, 1983), 85–119; Ernst H. Kantorowicz, *The King's Two Bodies* (Princeton: Princeton University Press, 1957), 42–52.

[10] Quentin Skinner, *The Foundations of Modern Political Thought*, vol. 1 (Cambridge: Cambridge University Press, 1978), 113–186.

[11] Anthony Grafton and Lisa Jardine, *From Humanism to the Humanities* (Cambridge, MA: Harvard University Press, 1986), xi–xvi, 1–28; L.D. Reynolds and N.G. Wilson, *Scribes and Scholars*, 4th ed. (Oxford: Oxford University Press, 2013), chaps. 3–4.

out inside a world that assumed Christian cosmology.[12] When Machiavelli reached for Roman examples, he was reaching through a Christian appropriation of Rome, not past it.

There is also a reading of Machiavelli as a deliberate subversive—a philosopher who understood exactly what he was doing in breaking with the Christian moral tradition and who concealed the radicalism of that break through careful rhetorical management.[13] On this reading, the surface accommodations to Christian language in his work are strategic cover; the real project was philosophical insurgency.

The difficulty is that if Machiavelli was breaking with a tradition, he needed somewhere else to stand. He needed a conceptual framework outside Christendom from which to conduct his critique. But there was nowhere else to stand. The Latin he thought in was Christian Latin. The political problems he analyzed were Christian civilization's problems. The audience he addressed was formed by Christian institutions. What looks like deliberate subversion is more accurately read as internal critique—the kind that can only be done from inside a tradition, by someone who knows it well enough to see where its self-understanding has diverged from its practice. Internal critics are often more devastating than external ones. They know where the weight is actually held.

This book develops that argument in full. The details and sources behind it appear in Chapter 3, which examines Machiavelli's epistemic formation directly. What matters here, at the outset, is the interpretive consequence: if Machiavelli is best read as an internal critic of Christendom, not an external opponent of it, then the relationship between his analysis and the civilization he analyzed is not one of distance and opposition — it is something closer to a surgeon operating on his own body.

What This Book Does

The book moves in six parts.

[12] Grafton and Jardine, *From Humanism to the Humanities*, 1–28; Paul Oskar Kristeller, *Renaissance Thought and Its Sources*, ed. Michael Mooney (New York: Columbia University Press, 1979), chaps. 1–3.
[13] Leo Strauss, *Thoughts on Machiavelli* (Glencoe, IL: Free Press, 1958), 9–14, 171–240.

The first establishes the entangled world—Machiavelli's biography, Christendom's political infrastructure, the linguistic and institutional formation that made his vocabulary what it was, and the texts he wrote once he had been stripped of everything except the capacity to analyze.

The second examines the architecture of Christendom in detail: competing authorities, the constitutional crisis of the Western Schism, and the human behavior that political institutions must work with regardless of what moral language surrounds them.

The third and fourth parts turn to the machinery of rule itself—office and mandate, executive power under necessity, indirect rule, reputation, faction, force, and legitimacy.

The fifth applies the analytical framework to scriptural narratives that Machiavelli's audience already knew: Judges, the institution of Kingship, the Maccabean revolt, the Pauline letters. These are not devotional readings. They are exercises in political analysis applied to texts that shaped the moral imagination of the civilization Machiavelli inhabited.

The sixth traces what survived the collapse of Christendom as a unified political order: the institutional forms, legal categories, and governance structures that migrated into modern political life under new names.

The book closes with an epilogue that applies the framework to the present. The mechanisms Machiavelli described are not historical curiosities. They are operating now, in institutions that readers of this book inhabit and lead.

A Note on Method

This book proceeds descriptively rather than prescriptively. It examines how power functioned in a Christian civilization without adjudicating the theological claims of that civilization. It draws on Machiavelli's analytic framework without endorsing his conclusions or treating his judgments as the last word. Description and endorsement are different things. Diagnosis is not a prescription.

Readers will bring different commitments to this material—theological, political, institutional. That is appropriate. The aim is not to produce agreement but to improve the quality of perception. Moral reasoning that operates on imagined conditions rather than actual ones does not produce good outcomes regardless of the sincerity behind it. Clarity about how institutions actually function is a precondition of responsible action within them, not an alternative to it.[14]

Machiavelli understood this. He did not write to make his readers cynical. He wrote to make them see. The Sack of Rome confirmed everything he had argued: that a civilization which mistakes moral consensus for institutional capacity will find, eventually, that its walls are thinner than it thought.

The army that crossed the Tiber that May was not composed of pagans or infidels. It was composed of Christians, led by the most powerful Christian ruler in the world, serving an emperor who bore the institutional title of Rome's Christian successor.[15] They destroyed the capital of the institution that had done more than any other to build the civilization they were dismantling. Machiavelli spent his life asking how this kept happening. This book attempts to explain what he found.

[14] Aquinas, *Summa Theologiae*, II–II, q. 47, a. 8.
[15] Chastel, *Sack of Rome*, 199–210.

PART I

One World: Machiavelli Inside Christendom

This part introduces a man and the world that formed him. They cannot be separated, and the five chapters that follow do not try. The argument is not that Christendom provides useful context for reading Machiavelli — that his realism becomes more legible when placed against the backdrop of his civilization. The argument is stronger: Christendom was constitutive of his analytical capacity. The schools that taught him, the Latin he wrote in, the rhetorical traditions he worked within, the moral vocabulary he deployed and redirected, the political problems that preoccupied him — all of it descended from institutions the Church had built. He did not observe Christendom. He thought inside it, with it, and finally about it, having been made by it into exactly the kind of observer capable of seeing what it was.

Chapter 1 establishes his biography with this entanglement foregrounded — not as an interesting detail but as the interpretive key to everything that follows. Chapter 2 describes Christendom as a political civilization, arguing that Christian institutions were not a moral overlay on top of political life but the operating system through which governance, law, welfare, and legitimacy functioned. Chapter 3 — the philological center of the part — traces what happened to Machiavelli's central terms (*virtù, fortuna, necessità, gloria*) during the thousand years they spent inside Christian theological and legal discourse before he inherited them. It argues that all three of the dominant scholarly readings — Skinner's civic humanism, Pocock's classical republicanism, Strauss's deliberate anti-Christianity — have misread the epistemic environment that formed him by presupposing a vantage point outside Christendom that was not available.[16] Chapter 4 examines what he actually wrote with those tools, and why the texts look different once their Christian institutional formation is taken seriously.

[16] Skinner, *Foundations*, vol. 1, 113–186; Pocock, *Machiavellian Moment*, 49–80; Strauss, *Thoughts on Machiavelli*, 9–14. (Full treatment in Ch. 3 footnotes [8]–[10].)

Chapter 5 shows how his redirected vocabulary functions analytically — what the *effectual truth* does once it is understood as a tradition's own language turned against the tradition's preferred consolations.

The interpretive claim connecting all five chapters can be stated plainly: you cannot understand Machiavelli without Christendom, and you cannot understand Christendom without Machiavelli. The first half of that claim is argued here, through biography, institutional history, and philology — showing how thoroughly his formation was shaped by the civilization he analyzed, and why no available scholarly framework that positions him as standing outside or against that civilization is adequate to the evidence. The second half is argued across the rest of the book — showing how his analytical vocabulary, applied to the specific mechanisms of Christian political civilization, makes visible what remains obscure when that civilization is examined only through its own self-understanding.

By the end of Part I, the reader holds a lens ground inside the tradition it is used to examine. That is not a limitation; it is what makes the lens sharp.

External critiques of Christendom's political mechanics have been conducted from many positions, by historians and political theorists who approached it as an object. What Machiavelli offers that those critiques cannot is the precision available only to the formed participant — someone who understood the gap between what the civilization claimed and what it did because he had spent a career managing that gap from the inside. His *effectual truth* was not a method imported from elsewhere. It was the name he gave to what service, failure, imprisonment, and exile had taught him about how power actually operates when the moral language runs out.

CHAPTER 1

WHO MACHIAVELLI WAS

Niccolò Machiavelli was born in 1469 into a world the Church had built. The Florence that formed him was Christian not as a matter of private devotion but as a matter of public infrastructure:[17] its schools, its laws, its administrative language, its moral vocabulary, its sense of what rulers owed their subjects and what subjects owed their rulers. He learned to read in institutions shaped by centuries of ecclesiastical transmission. He learned to write in a Latin that had been living inside Christian use for a thousand years before he touched it. When he entered public life, he entered a chancery whose rhetorical traditions descended from monastic letter-writing practice and whose every act of diplomacy unfolded within frameworks of Christian legitimacy. He did not observe Christendom from a distance. He was its product.

This matters for how we read him. Machiavelli is often encountered as a figure who broke with his world — a secular analyst in a religious age, a realist surrounded by moralists, a man who stripped away Christian pieties to reveal the political machinery underneath. That reading is seductive and wrong. His realism was possible only because he understood the civilization he was analyzing from the inside. The machinery he named was machinery he had operated. The gap he described between moral aspiration and political capacity was a gap he had watched open and widen across decades of service within Christian institutions. His thought did not transcend his context. It was produced by it.

Florence was among the most sophisticated urban centers in Europe. Its wealth derived from banking, commerce, and textile production.[18] Its influence extended through diplomatic, financial, and patronage networks across the Italian peninsula and beyond. Cultural prestige rested on art, architecture, and humanist learning that shaped European intellectual life for generations. Alongside this achievement, political order remained unstable. Republican ideals coexisted with

---

[17] Sebastian de Grazia, *Machiavelli in Hell* (Princeton: Princeton University Press, 1989), 3–8.

[18] Richard A. Goldthwaite, *The Economy of Renaissance Florence* (Baltimore: Johns Hopkins, 2009), 75–110.

oligarchic control. Constitutions were drafted, revised, and abandoned.[19] Councils convened and dissolved. Power shifted through faction, exile, and sudden reversal, never through settled law or orderly succession.

This volatility reflected the broader condition of the Italian peninsula at the close of the fifteenth century. Italy functioned as a mosaic of competing powers: city-republics, princely states, dynastic kingdoms, and the Papal States.[20] These regimes shared a Christian culture, a common legal inheritance, and a moral vocabulary of rule, yet authority and capacity rarely extended beyond local borders. Political power remained fragmented, contested, and provisional.

Christian rulers governed through a language of moral legitimacy amid constant uncertainty. Foreign armies crossed Italian borders with ease. French, Spanish, and imperial forces treated the peninsula as a strategic corridor, not a sovereign space. Wealth attracted invasion, and internal division enabled it. Italy's political sophistication — its diplomacy, legal maneuvering, and ceremonial authority — proved insufficient against coordinated military force capable of decisive action.

This environment shaped Machiavelli's formation. He entered public life within a political system that repeatedly failed to defend itself despite administrative complexity and moral seriousness. Across years of service, he encountered at close range the gap between institutional aspiration and political outcome.

Foreign intervention dominated these decades. Italian states relied heavily on mercenary armies, whose loyalty followed payment, not allegiance.[21] These forces avoided decisive engagement, shifted sides opportunistically, and consumed vast resources while providing limited security. Machiavelli's hostility to mercenaries emerged from this experience. A state that lacked command over its own enforcement, he concluded, could not preserve its laws, its independence, or its legitimacy. Military weakness was not a technical deficiency. It was a political vulnerability with civilizational consequences — a failure of institutional design that no amount of moral seriousness could compensate for.

---

[19] Najemy, *A History of Florence; Rubinstein*, Government of Florence under the Medici.

[20] Michael Mallett and Christine Shaw, *The Italian Wars 1494–1559* (Harlow: Pearson, 2012), ch 1.

[21] Machiavelli, *The Prince*, chaps. 12–14; Mallett, *Mercenaries and Their Masters*, 180–190.

◆

To understand Machiavelli's political thought, one must understand what the papacy actually was in his world — not as a theological institution observed from a distance, but as the central organizing force of the civilization he inhabited.[22] The pope was simultaneously the spiritual head of Western Christendom and the ruler of a territorial state with armies, revenues, alliances, and dynastic ambitions. Moral authority and political strategy were not two separate things that happened to coexist in the same office. They were structurally fused. Papal decisions about doctrine and papal decisions about war were made by the same person using the same institutional infrastructure, drawing on the same fund of legitimacy.

This fusion was not a corruption of Christianity's original purpose. It was the predictable result of a thousand years in which Christian institutions had accumulated governance responsibilities.[23] The Church administered education. It ran the welfare system. It supplied the trained personnel on whom secular rulers depended for administration, legal reasoning, and diplomacy. It provided the moral vocabulary through which authority was justified and contested. By Machiavelli's time, you could not separate the political system of Christian Europe from its ecclesiastical infrastructure any more than you could separate a building from its foundations. They were the same thing.

Machiavelli did not observe this from outside it. His entire analytical formation occurred within it. The problems that preoccupied him — faction, mercenaries, the fragility of republics, the gap between moral language and political survival — were the specific problems of a civilization the Church had built and in which the Church remained a major political actor. When he analyzed the papacy critically, as he frequently did, he was not criticizing an external institution. He was conducting an internal audit of the civilization that had formed his capacity to think.

◆

Among the figures Machiavelli observed most closely was Cesare Borgia — and Borgia repays careful attention precisely because his career makes visible what is

[22] Paolo Prodi, *The Papal Prince: One Body and Two Souls* (Cambridge: Cambridge University Press, 1987), 1–26.
[23] Berman, *Law and Revolution*, 85–165.

usually obscured.[24] Borgia was the illegitimate son of Pope Alexander VI, and his campaign to consolidate power in central Italy was not a political project that happened to have a papal family connection. It was a project whose entire foundation was papal. His military resources came from his father's revenues. His diplomatic leverage derived from his father's authority to grant and withhold spiritual sanction. His ability to eliminate rivals, absorb territories, and build administrative structures in the Romagna depended at every stage on the institutional weight of the papacy behind him.

When Alexander VI died in 1503, Cesare moved quickly to secure his position, striking a bargain with Cardinal Giuliano della Rovere — who had spent the previous decade in exile opposing the Borgia papacy — to support his election in exchange for confirmation as captain of the papal forces and lord of his Romagnol territories. Della Rovere was elected unanimously as Julius II on 1 November 1503, the fastest conclave on record. Machiavelli, who was in Rome at the time as a Florentine envoy, watched the entire sequence unfold.[25]

Within a month, Julius declared that his duty as head of the Church took precedence over any earlier commitment.[26] He forced Cesare to surrender his fortresses as the price of being allowed to leave Rome, and set about recovering the papal territories that Cesare's campaigns had seized in his father's name. Borgia's power collapsed with a speed that revealed exactly how thoroughly it had rested on ecclesiastical foundations — and how completely the logic of office could override the logic of personal agreement. The same institutional machinery that had made Cesare's rise possible unmade it the moment the office changed hands.

This is what Christendom looked like from the inside. Political power and ecclesiastical power were not separate systems that occasionally cooperated or conflicted. They were one system with two vocabularies. A man could simultaneously be a cardinal and a military commander, a spiritual authority and a territorial prince, because the civilization had been built in a way that made those roles continuous, not contradictory.

---

[24] Machiavelli, *The Prince*, chap. 7; Bradford, *Cesare Borgia*, 99–125.

[25] Christine Shaw, *Julius II: The Warrior Pope* (Oxford: Blackwell, 1993), 120–122; Niccolò Machiavelli, *Legazioni e Commissarie*, ed. S. Bertelli (Milan, 1964), vol. II, 590.

[26] Shaw, *Julius II*, 130. Julius told the Venetian ambassador that he could not, "with honour nor in good conscience," allow others to take the lands of the Church — a declaration that effectively voided his promises to Cesare.

Machiavelli observed Borgia as a case study in political skill — the decisive action, the strategic use of force, the management of appearances. But he observed him within a world where that skill operated through institutions the Church had created and continued to animate. The lesson Machiavelli drew was not about secular politics operating despite religious context. It was about politics operating through a civilization that was Christian to its structural foundations.

Borgia's eventual failure resulted from adverse circumstances as much as from strategic limitation. His rise and fall revealed both the possibilities and the limits of political skill in a world governed by contingency, not moral intention — but also, crucially, in a world where the most consequential single institution was the papacy, and where losing control of that institution meant losing the ground on which everything else stood.

✦

Machiavelli's own career ended abruptly in 1512, when the Medici family returned to power in Florence with Spanish support. The republic collapsed. Machiavelli was dismissed from office, imprisoned, and tortured on suspicion of conspiracy.[27] After his release, exclusion from public service followed. For a man whose identity was bound to political participation and institutional responsibility — who understood himself through his function within the machinery of a Christian republic — this rupture was total. It separated experience from action, knowledge from use.

During this enforced withdrawal, Machiavelli turned to writing. Removed from the institutions he had served and the problems he had managed, he subjected political action itself to sustained analysis. The Prince emerged from this period [28]— a compressed memorandum addressed to a Medici ruler attempting to consolidate authority in a city whose institutional loyalties remained divided, within a peninsula that had not found a way to resist foreign invasion, within a civilization whose moral language and political capacity had been visibly diverging for decades. It was not a work of philosophy composed in tranquility. It was a practitioner's analysis written in exile by someone who had spent fourteen years watching the gap between aspiration and reality widen.

---

[27] Najemy, *A History of Florence*, 439–448; Viroli, Machiavelli, 91–99.

[28] Machiavelli, *The Prince*, dedicatory letter; Skinner, *Machiavelli*, 17–23.

Conflict, instability, and failure appeared in that analysis as ordinary conditions, not anomalies — because for Machiavelli they were ordinary conditions. He had not observed them from a scholarly distance. He had managed them, been shaped by them, and ultimately been destroyed by them. The analytical posture of The Prince, its refusal of consolation and its insistence on examining what institutions actually produce instead of what they claim to pursue, reflects this formation directly.

What emerges from this biographical account is the book's governing claim, which should be stated plainly here at the outset: Machiavelli's mind was made by a civilization the Church built, and that civilization cannot be fully understood without the diagnostic he performed on it. His problems were the problems of that civilization under strain. His vocabulary — the Latin he thought in, the moral categories he redirected, the political concepts he sharpened — was a Christian vocabulary, formed by centuries of theological and institutional use before he inherited it. And yet Christendom, precisely because it was so thoroughly moralized, resisted the kind of honest examination Machiavelli practiced. The civilization needed a diagnostician who could see its political mechanisms without flinching, and it produced one. This book examines both: the world that made his analysis possible, and the analysis that makes that world intelligible.

By the time of his death in 1527, Italy remained divided and exposed. The Sack of Rome that same year — described in this book's Introduction — confirmed what Machiavelli had spent his career arguing: that a civilization which mistakes moral language for institutional capacity will find, eventually, that the walls are thinner than it thought. The tensions he analyzed did not recede after his death. They intensified, and their consequences are still being worked through.

To encounter Machiavelli, then, is to encounter a witness formed by the civilization he was witnessing. He observed Christian civilization confronting the limits of its institutional arrangements from inside those arrangements, and described without consolation how governance functioned when ideals met survival. The description endures because the problem endures. The gap he named is still the gap that breaks institutions — including the ones his readers inhabit and lead.

CHAPTER 2

Christendom as Political Infrastructure

The preceding chapter described a man formed by a civilization. This chapter describes the civilization. They cannot be understood separately — and that entanglement is not incidental to this book's argument. It is the argument. Machiavelli's analytical categories, his problems, his vocabulary, his audience, and his political instincts were all products of the world examined here. What follows is not background; it is the ground on which everything he wrote stands.

The term Christendom is often used imprecisely, applied interchangeably to Christian belief, to medieval Europe as a cultural period, or to a generalized religious past. What matters politically is more specific.[29] In this book, Christendom names a civilizational arrangement: a political environment in which Christian institutions, moral language, and authority structures were embedded in the ordinary functioning of public life. Not as decoration. Not as ideology layered over a secular political reality underneath. But as the framework within which public life operated.

This distinction is more than semantic. Christianity names a religion ordered toward theological truth and salvific ends. Christendom names a social order in which Christian institutions supplied administrative capacity, legal frameworks, educational systems, welfare mechanisms, and the moral vocabulary through which authority was justified and contested.[30] It can be examined as a political structure without adjudicating its theological truth claims, just as Roman law can be studied independently of Roman religion. Machiavelli assumes precisely this mode of examination. He writes about Christian Europe as a political reality, not a theological project — not because he was dismissive of its theology, but because he was ruthlessly attentive to how its institutions actually functioned under pressure.

[29] Berman, *Law and Revolution*, 1–44.

[30] Southern, *Western Society and the Church*, 15–60; Skinner, *Foundations*, vol. 1, 113–160.

Christendom emerged gradually as Christianity moved from marginal movement to legally recognized faith and eventually to dominant public authority. As this occurred, Christian institutions accumulated responsibilities extending far beyond worship. Bishops exercised judicial authority.[31] Church courts governed marriage, inheritance, vows, and obligation. Monasteries organized labor, preserved knowledge, and structured local economies. Education, charity, and moral regulation increasingly passed through ecclesiastical channels. Over time, these functions hardened into infrastructure.

By the late medieval period, Christendom functioned as a shared operating environment, not a unified polity.[32] Kings, princes, city councils, popes, and imperial authorities contested sovereignty, jurisdiction, and supremacy. Despite persistent conflict, these actors competed within a common symbolic and institutional framework. Authority was articulated in Christian terms even when conduct diverged from Christian norms. Political conflict unfolded through Christendom's moral grammar, never outside it.

This framework shaped how power was experienced and understood. Rulers presented themselves through the language of duty, justice, order, conscience, and divine sanction. Subjects encountered the rule as morally intelligible even when it was resented. Legitimacy was never automatic, but it was recognizable. In political life, recognizability often matters more than sincerity, because obedience depends less on belief than on intelligibility.

Christendom's most consequential feature was the overlap of authority. Secular rulers appealed to divine sanction. The Church asserted spiritual supremacy. Cities defended ancient liberties. Noble families claimed hereditary privilege.[33] Guilds protected economic rights. Each drew on the same Christian moral vocabulary to justify its claims. Conflict arose because this symbolic inheritance was shared. Rival authorities appealed to identical resources to legitimate incompatible demands.

This overlap both stabilized and strained political life. Shared moral language allowed power to be interpreted and contested without immediate collapse. At the

---

[31] Berman, *Law and Revolution*, 1–44; Brundage, *Medieval Canon Law*, 65-68.
[32] Tierney, *Crisis of Church and State*, 1–20.
[33] Strayer, *Medieval Origins of the Modern State*, 35–60.

same time, moralization intensified conflict. Political disagreement became moral disagreement, and opponents were framed as unjust, impious, or corrupt. Christendom rendered conflict meaningful even as it made compromise more difficult.

Religion's role within this system was primarily infrastructural. Christian institutions organized education, administered charity, structured time, shaped law, and mediated social conflict.[34] The Church functioned as one of the principal mechanisms through which society operated. Challenges to ecclesiastical authority therefore disrupted administration, welfare, and legitimacy simultaneously.

From a modern vantage point, this arrangement can be difficult to perceive. Contemporary societies tend to separate belief from governance and morality from administration. In Christendom, religious institutions operated as core systems of political order. Removing them would not have clarified authority. It would have dismantled it.

Over centuries, the Church became the most stable, literate, and territorially continuous institution in Europe.[35] Dynasties rose and fell. Borders shifted. Cities were destroyed and rebuilt. Ecclesiastical offices endured. Records were kept. Norms were preserved. Expectations stabilized. For political life, this continuity mattered more than theology. Where secular authority was episodic and personal, the Church supplied temporal depth.

Political authority depended on this depth. Rule could not outlast individual rulers without institutions capable of memory and transmission. Continuity — not charisma — was the scarce resource — and across much of Latin Europe the Church had long supplied it. By Machiavelli's lifetime, however, some of Christendom's formative functions were no longer housed exclusively in ecclesiastical institutions. In the Italian city-states especially, communal governments, private masters, and humanist schools had assumed a larger role in training the literate personnel on whom political life depended.[36]

---

[34] Berman, *Law and Revolution*, 85–164.

[35] Strayer, *Medieval Origins of the Modern State*, 9.

[36] Grendler, *Schooling in Renaissance Italy*, 11–14, 29.

Education illustrates the shift clearly. Monasteries and cathedral schools had once been central to the preservation and transmission of learning. But by the late medieval and Renaissance periods in Italy, pre-university schooling was increasingly carried by civic and lay institutions responsive to the needs of urban government, commerce, and diplomacy.[37] Clerics were still trained by ecclesiastical bodies, and church institutions remained important to the broader world of learning. Yet the administrators, jurists, secretaries, physicians, and diplomats of Machiavelli's age were often formed in schools sponsored by communes or taught by independent masters, not in cathedral classrooms.[38]

This did not place education outside Christendom. The languages, textual canons, moral assumptions, and institutional purposes that structured such schooling were still products of a civilization shaped by Christendom and sustained in large part by the Church. Latin remained the language of law, administration, and diplomacy. Rhetoric, textual interpretation, and moral reasoning continued to develop within an intellectual world saturated by Christian inheritance, even where instruction had become more civic than ecclesiastical in administration.[39] Political authority therefore depended on a knowledge system that had partly differentiated from direct church control without ceasing to belong to Christendom's broader order.

Rulers and city councils depended on personnel formed within this mixed system. Even where secular authorities funded schools more directly, they did not create an entirely new grammar of rule from nothing. They inherited and repurposed one already in place. Education thus reveals an important truth about Christendom: its infrastructure was not limited to institutions formally governed by the Church. It also included the durable moral, linguistic, and administrative patterns that survived institutional migration and continued to shape how power was exercised and judged.

Charity functioned in a similar way. Care for the poor, the sick, widows, orphans, pilgrims, and the displaced was institutionalized through hospitals, confraternities, parish relief, and alms systems administered by religious bodies. This charity stabilized political life by absorbing social shock. In societies

---

37 Grendler, *Schooling in Renaissance Italy*, 6–12.
38 Grendler, *Schooling in Renaissance Italy*, 13–14.
39 Grendler, *Schooling in Renaissance Italy*, 111–14.

vulnerable to famine, plague, and war, unmanaged suffering translated quickly into unrest.

Relief was morally framed and selectively administered. Need was assessed. Deservingness was judged. Assistance reinforced norms and hierarchies even as it alleviated hardship. Charity governed behavior as much as it relieved it. Political authority benefited from this arrangement without directly administering it. Social peace was maintained through institutions that appeared moral instead of coercive — and that appearance carried weight.

Law bore the same imprint. Canon law governed marriage, legitimacy, inheritance, contracts, vows, and moral conduct. Ecclesiastical courts adjudicated disputes central to social continuity.[40] Jurisdiction overlapped with secular courts, and conflict was frequent. This complexity allowed governance to reach domains inaccessible to force alone. Even secular law drew heavily on theological categories, framing justice as restitution, crime as moral transgression, and obedience as duty.

As a result, obedience was experienced as conformity to a moral order, not mere submission to power. Power that relies solely on fear requires constant enforcement. Power that is morally intelligible governs through habit.

Ritual completed the structure. Calendars organized time around holy days, fasts, and feasts. Public ceremonies — processions, coronations, oaths, and liturgies — did more than express belief. They enacted legitimacy.[41] Through repetition, ritual trained perception so that authority appeared familiar, predictable, and continuous.

Moral language also supplied the primary grammar of political life. Concepts such as duty, honor, sin, conscience, justice, sacrifice, and salvation shaped how power was justified and how resistance was articulated. Rulers spoke in the language of responsibility. Critics accused them of failure. Political conflict unfolded within a shared symbolic field that structured struggle without eliminating it.

Taken together — education, charity, law, ritual, and moral narrative — these elements formed the process through which legitimacy was produced. Rule came to be experienced as rightful, not merely effective. Legitimacy emerged from the

---

[40] Brundage, *Medieval Canon Law*, 58-60; Berman, *Law and Revolution*, 120.

[41] Kantorowicz, *The King's Two Bodies*, 285-286.

integration of institutions into a coherent moral environment that shaped expectation and habit over time.

This process was cumulative and fragile. When religious institutions reinforced political authority, rule appeared stable. When they fractured, withdrew support, or became contested, authority weakened rapidly. Power that lost moral credibility faced disbelief as much as opposition.

✦

There is one further consequence of this picture that bears stating directly, because it governs everything that follows in this book. Christendom was not simply the political environment Machiavelli observed and analyzed from some neutral vantage point outside it. It was the environment that formed his capacity to observe at all.

The Latin in which he was educated and wrote had been shaped by a millennium of classical and Christian transmission before he inherited it. The rhetorical traditions that made him an effective writer were transmitted through the humanist Latin culture of Renaissance Italy, itself built on a long medieval and Christian inheritance. The moral and political categories he worked with — virtue, necessity, fortune, glory, honor — came to him through a civilization shaped by centuries of classical, theological, legal, and educational development before he redirected them toward political analysis.

The problems that preoccupied him were the specific problems of a civilization long shaped by Christendom and sustained in large part by the Church: how to maintain authority in a moralized world, how to preserve legitimacy when enforcement and moral language pull apart, how to govern human beings whose behavior routinely defies the ideals used to justify ruling them. He could not have formulated those problems without the formation Christendom gave him, and the analytical tools he developed to address them had, in a real sense, been prepared by that civilization in advance.

This is not a diminishment of his originality. Internal critics are often more penetrating than external ones precisely because they understand the system they are examining from the inside. Machiavelli's realism was possible because he had inhabited the gap between Christendom's self-understanding and its political practice across a career of direct service. The civilization that formed him also, eventually, gave him everything he needed to diagnose it.

Machiavelli understood this infrastructure with unusual clarity. He observed how rulers relied on religious institutions for legitimacy,[42] how they negotiated with ecclesiastical authority, and how moral language could stabilize power or undermine it when mishandled. He treated religion as institutional reality with causal force, never as illusion or mere manipulation.

To rule in Christendom was therefore to rule within a religiously organized environment, whether one sought to uphold it, reform it, or navigate its constraints. Religion functioned as a foundation of power. Political authority that misunderstood this environment failed not through moral error but through structural misreading.

This is the world Machiavelli analyzed. Christendom is the environment his concepts presuppose — and more than that, the environment that produced his capacity to form those concepts. To mistake it for doctrine is to misread him. To treat it as mere background is to miss the depth of the entanglement. His realism begins here: with a civilization that taught him, employed him, constrained him, and finally gave him a subject worthy of his full attention.

[42] Machiavelli, *The Prince*, ch. 11; Skinner, *Machiavelli* (Oxford, 2000), 42–46.

CHAPTER 3

The World That Made His Words

When Niccolò Machiavelli reached for a word, he reached into a thousand years of Christian use. This is the interpretive key to everything he wrote, not a minor biographical detail.

The political vocabulary that structures his analysis — *virtù*, *fortuna*, *necessità*, *gloria*, the *effectual truth* — did not arrive to him clean from Roman antiquity. These terms had been living inside Christian theological and legal discourse for ten centuries before he inherited them. Aquinas had built an entire moral psychology around *virtus*. Boethius had made *fortuna* into the central problem of a providential cosmos. Augustine had subjected *gloria* to an extended theological critique that no educated reader of Machiavelli's time could have forgotten. When Machiavelli deployed these terms, his readers heard that history. The tension his writing generates — the unsettling friction between his vocabulary and his conclusions — is partly produced by that hearing. He was using inherited Christian categories to reach conclusions the tradition had refused to draw.

This chapter examines how that inheritance worked. It proceeds in three movements. The first describes the infrastructure of literacy in Machiavelli's world — the institutional machinery through which texts, Latin, and rhetorical training were transmitted. The second traces what happened to the specific terms Machiavelli used most during the thousand years they spent inside Christian culture. The third draws the interpretive consequence: scholars who read Machiavelli as a secular recovery of classical antiquity, or as a deliberate philosophical insurgent against Christianity, have misread the epistemic environment that formed him. He was neither. He was something more interesting: an internal diagnostician whose tools were the tradition's own.

I. The Infrastructure of Literacy

Before the printing press, text production in Europe was overwhelmingly ecclesiastical. This statement requires emphasis because its full implication is easily underestimated. It means not merely that the Church produced religious texts, but that the Church produced almost all texts. The manuscript traditions that preserved classical Latin authors — Livy, Cicero, Virgil, Sallust, the writers Machiavelli knew and loved — survived because monks copied them, cathedral libraries stored them, and clerical scholars annotated them across generations. The antiquity Machiavelli reached toward had been filtered, preserved, and transmitted by Christian institutions for a thousand years before it reached him.

The grammar schools of fifteenth-century Florence confirm this picture in detail. Paul Grendler's exhaustive study of schooling in Renaissance Italy documents what Florentine boys actually read and how they were taught to read it.[43] The foundational texts were Christian: the Psalter served as a primary reading primer, and students encountered Latin first through liturgical and devotional material before progressing to classical authors. The *Disticha Catonis*, a standard elementary text, had been transmitted through medieval Christian commentary that had thoroughly moralized its content. Even as the curriculum expanded to include Cicero, Virgil, and the historians, it did so within institutions — schools attached to churches, run by clerics or men formed in clerical culture — that understood the classical inheritance as continuous with, not opposed to, Christian formation.

The rhetorical tradition that made Machiavelli an effective writer carries the same institutional signature. The *ars dictaminis* — the formal art of Latin composition that governed diplomatic correspondence, legal documents, and official communications — was developed in Italian Benedictine monasteries and cathedral schools during the eleventh and twelfth centuries.[44] Its foundational theorists were monks and cathedral masters. Its manuals were produced in ecclesiastical contexts. By the time this tradition reached the Florentine chancery where Machiavelli served, it had been in continuous institutional use for four centuries — but its origins were monastic, and its formal structures retained that inheritance. When Machiavelli composed diplomatic dispatches and official memoranda, he was working within a rhetorical tradition the Church had built.

---

[43] Paul F. Grendler, *Schooling in Renaissance Italy: Literacy and Learning, 1300–1600* (Baltimore: Johns Hopkins University Press, 1989), 142–161.

[44] James J. Murphy, *Rhetoric in the Middle Ages* (Berkeley: University of California Press, 1974), 194–205.

The humanist movement did not change this picture as much as it is often assumed to. The early humanists who shaped the intellectual culture Machiavelli inherited worked within and for Christian institutional structures. Petrarch, often called the first humanist, was in minor holy orders. His passion for classical texts was framed within an explicitly Christian providential worldview — he read Roman history as a story whose meaning was ultimately illuminated by Christian revelation. Boccaccio, his successor, maintained close ties to the Church throughout his life. The Florentine Platonic Academy under Ficino, which did so much to shape the intellectual environment of Machiavelli's Florence, was funded by the Medici but led by a man who was a priest, whose life's work was a synthesis of Platonic philosophy and Christian theology, and who understood the recovery of classical learning as a deepening of Christian culture, not a departure from it.

Grafton and Jardine's account of humanist reading practices reinforces this picture.[45] The humanists did not read classical texts as secular documents arriving from a pagan world hermetically sealed from Christian influence. They read them as texts that had survived within and been shaped by Christian manuscript traditions, through Christian interpretive frameworks, toward purposes that were understood as compatible with Christian formation. The *studia humanitatis* — grammar, rhetoric, poetry, history, moral philosophy — were understood as preparation for virtue in a Christian sense, as formation for civic and religious life simultaneously. They were not a secular curriculum. They were a Christian curriculum that had expanded to include more of antiquity.

What this means for reading Machiavelli is concrete. The formation that made him capable of writing The Prince was Christian institutional formation from beginning to end. There is no recoverable layer of his education or his rhetorical training that stands outside that formation. The question is not whether Christendom shaped his capacity to think and write — it did, entirely — but what he did with the tools that formation gave him.

[45] Anthony Grafton and Lisa Jardine, *From Humanism to the Humanities* (Cambridge, MA: Harvard University Press, 1986), xi–xvi, 1–28.

II. What Happened to Latin in a Thousand Years

A language does not stand still. Latin in the fifteenth century was not Latin in the first century BCE. The words were recognizably the same; what they carried had been fundamentally transformed by a millennium of use inside Christian theological, legal, and devotional culture. To read Machiavelli's key terms as recovered classical concepts is to ignore this transformation and to miss the specific charge they carried for his readers.

Virtù

Classical Latin *virtus* named something close to martial excellence — the quality of a man (*vir*) who acted effectively and courageously in the world. It was a civic and military concept, tied to the republic, to performance under pressure, to the capacity for decisive action in service of collective life. That concept was already complex and contested within the classical tradition itself.

By Machiavelli's time, *virtus* had traveled through Ambrose, who Christianized it as the quality that enables right moral action in conformity with divine order. Augustine subjected pagan *virtus* to an extended critique as a form of spiritual pride masquerading as excellence. Above all, Aquinas built an elaborate moral psychology around the concept.[46] For Aquinas, *virtus* named a stable disposition toward the good — an acquired excellence of character that inclined a person toward right action reliably, not occasionally. The cardinal virtues (prudence, justice, fortitude, temperance) and the theological virtues (faith, hope, charity) formed a comprehensive account of human excellence ordered toward both natural and supernatural ends.

When Machiavelli's readers encountered *virtù* in The Prince — applied to rulers who acted decisively even when that action violated conventional moral expectation, and evaluated not by its conformity to a moral order but by its political effects — they heard the Thomistic framework as the thing being departed from. The tension the word generates in his writing is not accidental. It is produced by the distance between what the word had meant for two centuries of scholastic theology and what Machiavelli was now doing with it. His readers

[46] Thomas Aquinas, *Summa Theologiae*, I–II, qq. 55–67. Augustine, *De civitate Dei*, V.12–20.

would have felt that distance immediately. It was a large part of what made him unsettling.

Fortuna

Classical *fortuna* was a goddess — the personification of chance, luck, and the unpredictable reversals of human life. She was not a systematic philosophical concept but a vivid mythological presence, depicted with a wheel that raised and lowered human fortunes arbitrarily. This figure survived into the medieval period, but she survived in permanent theological tension with a concept that had no real classical equivalent: *providentia*, divine providence.

Boethius's *Consolation of Philosophy*, written in prison awaiting execution in 524 CE and among the most widely read texts in medieval Europe, is essentially an extended meditation on this tension.[47] Lady Philosophy appears to the imprisoned Boethius to explain that what appears to be the arbitrary cruelty of Fortune is in fact embedded within a providential order that human reason can partially grasp and to which it can reconcile itself. Fortune's wheel is real — people are genuinely raised and cast down by circumstance — but it operates within a cosmos ordered by a divine intelligence that guarantees ultimate meaning even where immediate experience suggests only randomness.

This framework was the dominant context in which Machiavelli's educated readers understood *fortuna*. The Boethian synthesis had been absorbed into the medieval Christian worldview so thoroughly that the problem of fortune was experienced as a theological problem — a question about the relationship between contingency and providence, between human agency and divine order.

When Machiavelli argued in Chapter 25 of The Prince that fortune controls perhaps half of human affairs but that the other half is governed by human agency — and that fortune is like a river that can be contained by preparation — he was not recovering a Roman concept. He was intervening in a debate that had been running inside Christian culture for a thousand years. His central illustration was Julius II, the pope whose impetuous temperament Machiavelli had observed at close range during diplomatic missions to Rome and whose military campaigns he

[47] Boethius, *Consolation of Philosophy*, II.1–8; IV.6. Henry Chadwick, *Boethius* (Oxford: Clarendon Press, 1981), 223–230.

had accompanied as a Florentine envoy. His intervention was to insist that human agency could meaningfully contest fortune, and that waiting on providence was a political strategy that had demonstrably failed. The theological charge of that claim would have been audible to every reader he addressed.

Necessità

Necessity — the idea that circumstances can compel actions that ordinary moral reasoning would prohibit — had an extensive Christian theological history before Machiavelli used it. Within the natural law tradition that ran from through the canonists and into the political theology of the late medieval period, necessity (*necessitas*) was a recognized category that could modify moral obligations.[48] The just war tradition turned significantly on claims of necessity: force was justified when necessary to defend the common good, and the same act that would be criminal under normal conditions could be obligatory under conditions of extreme necessity. The tradition of reason of state (*ragion di stato*), which Machiavelli is often credited with inventing, was in fact being developed inside Christian political theology simultaneously by canon lawyers and political theologians grappling with the same problems he addressed.

Machiavelli's distinctive contribution was not to introduce necessity as a political category but to strip it of the natural law framework that had bounded its use. In the Christian tradition, necessity modified obligation but did not abolish it — it permitted otherwise-prohibited actions under extreme conditions while preserving the underlying moral order. Machiavelli treats necessity as a standing condition of political life, not an exceptional circumstance, and he does not reinstate the natural law framework afterward. This is what made his treatment radical to his readers. They recognized the category. They recognized that he had removed its theological scaffolding.

Gloria

No term in Machiavelli's vocabulary had been more thoroughly processed by the Christian tradition than *gloria*. Roman civic *gloria* — the honor earned through

[48] Brian Tierney, The Idea of Natural Rights (Atlanta: Scholars Press, 1997), 73–77; James Turner Johnson, Just War Tradition and the Restraint of War (Princeton, 1981), ch. 5.

military achievement, public service, and political greatness — was subjected to one of the most extended and influential critiques in Christian intellectual history: the first five books of Augustine's *City of God*.[49] Augustine argued that Roman *gloria* was a form of spiritual pride — a desire for human praise that substituted an earthly reward for the love of God that should orient all human action. The Romans achieved great things, Augustine acknowledged, but they achieved them for the wrong reasons, and their earthly glory was their only reward.

This critique was not a minor theological aside. It was foundational to how Christian culture understood political achievement, civic honor, and the relationship between worldly success and genuine human excellence. When Machiavelli rehabilitated gloria as a legitimate and even central motivation for political action — arguing that the desire for lasting fame and honor was a productive force that political systems should cultivate instead of suppress — he was reversing a position Augustine had argued with extraordinary force and that had shaped Christian political culture for a millennium. His readers knew exactly what he was doing. The rehabilitation of gloria was not a recovery of Rome. It was a direct argument with Augustine.

III. What the Standard Readings Miss

The foregoing analysis has a direct implication for how Machiavelli's relationship to the Christian tradition should be understood — and that implication runs against the three most influential scholarly frameworks that have shaped his reception.

Quentin Skinner's influential account places Machiavelli within a tradition of Renaissance civic humanism that he treats as a meaningful alternative to medieval Christian political theology.[50] On this reading, the humanists recovered a classical republican vocabulary — centered on civic virtue, liberty, and the active political life — that offered something genuinely different from the Augustinian and Thomistic frameworks that had dominated medieval political thought.

---

[49] Augustine, *De civitate Dei*, I–V, esp. V.12–20; R.A. Markus, *Saeculum* (Cambridge: Cambridge University Press, 1970), 54–58.
[50] Skinner, *Foundations*, vol. 1, 113–186; Skinner, *Machiavelli: A Very Short Introduction* (Oxford, 2000), 48–72.

Machiavelli represents the most rigorous and unsentimental development of this civic humanist tradition.

The difficulty is institutional, not philosophical. Skinner's civic humanism requires a tradition that operated outside or against Christian culture — a space where something genuinely secular was being recovered. But as the preceding sections have shown, no such space existed. The humanists worked within Christian institutions, were formed in Christian educational structures, served Christian patrons, and understood their project as compatible with, not opposed to, Christian formation. The rhetorical traditions they drew on had been developed in Benedictine monasteries. The manuscript traditions they mined had been preserved in cathedral libraries. The universities where their ideas circulated were Church institutions. Civic humanism was a development within Christendom, not an exit from it — and Machiavelli's formation was thoroughly shaped by that fact.

J.G.A. Pocock's *The Machiavellian Moment* offers a more sophisticated reading that tracks Machiavelli's political thought as a response to a specifically classical problem: how a republic sustains itself against the corruption that time inevitably brings.[51] The tension between *virtù* and *fortuna* in this reading is understood as a reworking of the Roman civic problem of time and decay. Pocock's analysis is illuminating and his scholarship formidable. But his account treats the classical inheritance as if it arrived to Machiavelli clean — as if the *virtù/fortuna* tension were a problem Machiavelli was recovering from antiquity, not one he was inheriting through a thousand years of Christian transformation.

The anxiety about *fortuna* that structures Machiavelli's thought is not a recovered Roman problem. It is the Boethian problem — the theological problem of contingency within a providential cosmos — wearing Roman clothes. The specific form that problem takes in Machiavelli's work, the particular urgency it carries, the nature of the solution he proposes, all of this makes sense as a response to a world where providence was the governing cosmological assumption and where the repeated political failures of Christian civilization had made that assumption increasingly difficult to sustain. Pocock's reading captures the classical

[51] Pocock, *Machiavellian Moment*.

structure of Machiavelli's response without capturing its Christian existential stakes.

Leo Strauss's reading is the most directly opposed to the argument of this book.[52] Strauss treats Machiavelli as a deliberate and philosophically serious anti-Christian thinker — one of the founders of modernity precisely because he consciously broke with the Christian moral tradition and worked to establish an alternative on pagan philosophical foundations. The esoteric dimension of Strauss's reading holds that Machiavelli knew exactly what he was doing in departing from Christian morality, that he concealed the radicalism of this departure through careful rhetorical management, and that his surface accommodations to Christian language are strategic cover, not genuine engagement.

The problem with this reading is not that it claims Machiavelli was doing something radical — he was — but that it requires him to have had somewhere else to stand. An esoteric break from Christianity presupposes a conceptual framework available outside Christendom from which the break could be conducted and to which the thinker could retreat. But the preceding sections have shown that no such framework was available to Machiavelli. His conceptual vocabulary was Christian Latin vocabulary. His rhetorical formation was ecclesiastical in origin. His problems were the problems of a Christian civilization. His audience was formed by Christian institutions. There was no Archimedean point outside Christendom from which his supposed subversion could have been organized.

What Strauss reads as deliberate anti-Christian esotericism is more accurately described as internal critique — the kind of critique that is possible only from inside a tradition, by someone who understands its categories well enough to see where its self-understanding has diverged from its practice. Machiavelli did not reject the civilization that formed him. He diagnosed it. He described, with ruthless clarity, the gap between what Christian political civilization claimed to be and what it demonstrably was. That diagnosis is more disturbing than subversion, not less — because it implicates the tradition from within instead of attacking it from without.

---

[52] Strauss, *Thoughts on Machiavelli*, 9–14, 171–240; Mansfield, *Machiavelli's Virtue*, 281–294.

✦

The argument of this chapter can be stated simply: Machiavelli's words came from a Christian world, carried Christian history, and were heard by Christian readers who registered that history. The vocabulary of his analysis was not a neutral instrument he picked up and aimed at his subject. It was material saturated with meaning, and working with it — bending it, redirecting it, deploying it against the grain of its established uses — was itself a political and intellectual act of the first order.

This has a direct consequence for how his texts should be read, which is the subject of the next chapter. When Machiavelli describes a ruler who uses cruelty well, or insists that it is better to be feared than loved, or argues that a prince must know how to use both the lion and the fox — he is doing something more specific than offering a universal political theory. He is making arguments inside a tradition whose categories he has absorbed, whose failures he has witnessed, and whose vocabulary he is deliberately redirecting. Reading him outside that tradition produces a thinner and less accurate Machiavelli than the actual one.

The chapters that follow read him inside it. The world that made his words also made the problems those words were designed to address. Understanding both together is the interpretive commitment of this book.

CHAPTER 4

What Machiavelli Actually Wrote

The preceding chapter established how Machiavelli's words arrived to him: saturated with Christian theological and institutional history, formed by ecclesiastical educational structures, carrying meanings his readers would have recognized immediately. This chapter examines what he did with those words. His texts are the product of a mind entirely formed by Christian institutions, applied to political problems that were the specific problems of a Christian civilization. Reading them with that formation in view does not reduce their originality. It sharpens it.

Machiavelli's reputation rests primarily on two works: *The Prince* and the *Discourses on Livy*. These texts are often read as though they encompass his entire political thought. Read in isolation, they invite distortion.[53] Read alongside his letters, diplomatic dispatches, military writings, and historical works, they reveal a more demanding coherence: a sustained effort to describe how political power functioned within European Christendom under conditions of fragmentation, moral constraint, and persistent risk.

Machiavelli did not produce a political system in the philosophical sense. His work does not proceed from first principles toward a unified theory applied across cases. It develops instead through observation, comparison, and response to circumstance. Its coherence lies in posture, not doctrine: a commitment to begin political analysis with how institutions behave when tested.[54]

That posture is practical and institutional. Machiavelli writes as a practitioner reflecting on experience, drawing on service, failure, and proximity to power. His arguments proceed through cases — ancient and contemporary, successful and failed — treated as evidence, never as mere examples. He attends to leverage,

[53] Quentin Skinner, *Machiavelli: A Very Short Introduction* (Oxford: Oxford University Press, 2000), 1–3.

[54] Skinner, *Machiavelli*, 21–27; Pocock, *Machiavellian Moment*, 156–218.

credibility, enforcement, and timing. Political actions are evaluated by their effects over time, not by their conformity to professed ideals.

This approach accounts for the form of Machiavelli's writings. They were composed to address specific political problems as they arose: the consolidation of authority by a new ruler, the endurance of a republic across generations, the organization of military force, the management of factions, and the interpretation of historical collapse. What unites these texts is a consistent analytical lens applied across different institutional settings — never a fixed set of conclusions.

That lens was forged within a particular civilizational environment. Machiavelli wrote for a world in which Christianity supplied the dominant moral language of public life without producing political coherence. Princes ruled by divine sanction while relying on taxation, force, and alliance. Republics proclaimed liberty while struggling to manage inequality and faction. The Church asserted universal authority while operating as a territorial power among rivals. Machiavelli treats this environment as given and analyzes how Christian political institutions functioned under pressure.

❖

The Prince, written in 1513 after Machiavelli's removal from office, remains his most widely read work. Addressed to a Medici ruler consolidating power in Florence,[55] it takes the form of a practical memorandum. Its concerns are concrete: acquiring authority, securing obedience, managing alliances, avoiding destruction, and preserving the state. Its compressed style reflects its audience — a ruler confronting immediate danger with limited tolerance for abstraction.

The political situation it addresses was acute. Florence had lost its republican government. The Medici had returned with foreign support. Italian states faced collapse under external pressure, and no stable equilibrium existed. *The Prince* speaks to a ruler whose legitimacy was contested, whose institutions were fragile, and whose survival was uncertain. This context accounts for the urgency of the work and its refusal to offer moral reassurance.

The significance of *The Prince* lies in its method, not in any single recommendation. Machiavelli treats politics as an empirical discipline.[56] He begins

[55] Machiavelli, *The Prince*, dedicatory letter; Skinner, *Machiavelli*, 17–23.
[56] Machiavelli, *The Prince*, chap. 15; Pocock, *Machiavellian Moment*, 156–218.

with observed regularities in human behavior under constraint and examines outcomes instead of intentions. Across historical cases, he asks what actions reveal about the conditions under which authority is maintained or lost.

This framework clarifies his treatment of violence. Machiavelli evaluates force by its political consequences. He distinguishes between severity that consolidates authority and cruelty that generates hatred and revolt.[57] His concern centers on whether actions secure order over time or accelerate collapse.

It is worth noting, given the analysis of Chapter 3, that this treatment of violence is conducted entirely in the vocabulary of a tradition that had spent centuries debating the just use of force — the natural law and canon law discussions of necessity, proportion, and legitimate authority that shaped the moral formation of every reader *The Prince* addressed. Machiavelli was not introducing violence as a political category. He was stripping the category of the theological scaffolding that had constrained its use and examining what it did when left to operate on purely political logic.

✦

The *Discourses on Livy* extend this analytic posture to republican government. Where *The Prince* examines the founding and preservation of authority in a single ruler, the *Discourses* analyze the endurance of free states across generations.[58] Drawing on Roman history, Machiavelli examines faction, law, office, and popular participation. Conflict appears as a permanent feature of collective life. The central question concerns whether institutions can contain and direct it.

In the Roman Republic, Machiavelli identifies an approach to institutional design that formalized social conflict instead of attempting to eliminate it. Tension between patricians and plebeians generated offices, laws, and procedures that expanded participation while preserving authority. Tribunes, assemblies, and legal appeals gave rivalry form. Order emerged through structured contest, not enforced harmony.

The Rome Machiavelli draws on in the Discourses is not Rome recovered from primary sources through independent scholarly work. It is Rome as transmitted

---

[57] Machiavelli, *The Prince*, chaps. 8, 17–19.

[58] Machiavelli, *Discourses*, I.2–6; Pocock, *Machiavellian Moment*, 175–190.

through Livy's text, which had arrived to him through a thousand years of Christian manuscript copying and annotation, read in a humanist culture that understood Roman civic history as providentially continuous with Christian civilization. When he uses Rome to argue against the political failures of his own time, he is working with a version of antiquity that Christendom had already processed and shaped. His intervention is to draw from that processed inheritance conclusions the tradition had refused to draw.

The lesson Machiavelli draws is structural. Political stability depends on the organization of struggle, not its absence. Institutions fail when they lack the capacity to process disagreement without collapse. When opposition lacks lawful outlets, it seeks unlawful ones. When ambition is excluded, it becomes conspiratorial. When power accumulates without counterbalance, resentment grows until containment breaks down.

Machiavelli also attends closely to institutional decay. Political forms harden over time. Offices accumulate privilege.[59] Procedures designed to restrain power become instruments of domination. Reform becomes increasingly difficult as it threatens entrenched interests. This erosion proceeds gradually and often escapes notice until capacity has already weakened.

◆

His other writings reinforce this analysis. His diplomatic dispatches track intention, leverage, military capacity, and credibility, recording what political positions permit actors to do.[60] His military treatise, *The Art of War*, treats control over force as a foundational political institution, never a technical specialty. Dependence on mercenaries, he argues, undermines autonomy; authority over arms and authority over law remain inseparable.

His *History of Florence* applies the same diagnostic lens to his own city. It traces factional struggle, constitutional instability, and the recurring cycle of reform and collapse that shaped Florentine life. The work seeks explanation, not vindication, showing how political forms shape behavior over time and why reforms falter when institutional foundations remain weak.

---

[59] Machiavelli, *Discourses*, I.17–18, I.49, III.1; Pocock, *Machiavellian Moment*.

[60] Machiavelli, *Legazioni*, vol 2; cited in Maurizio Viroli, *Machiavelli* (Oxford: Oxford University Press, 1998), 61–67, 71–72.

Debate over the tone and intent of Machiavelli's writing has persisted since the sixteenth century. Some readers emphasize satire; others emphasize instruction.[61] The distinction matters less than his audience. Machiavelli wrote for rulers operating under real constraints, not for abstract moral reflection. His examples draw from popes, kings, generals, and republics. His concerns remain operational.

Reading Machiavelli with care requires avoiding two common distortions: treating him as an advocate of cruelty or as a theorist who dissolves politics from morality altogether. His work instead offers diagnosis. He describes a civilization under strain and insists that serious accounts of governance begin with what that strain produces.

❖

This insistence — that political analysis must begin with what institutions actually produce instead of what they claim to pursue — is what has made Machiavelli enduringly controversial. It is also what has made him enduringly misread.

The dominant scholarly traditions have read him as a figure who broke with the Christian world he inhabited: who recovered classical republicanism as a secular alternative to medieval political theology, or who reconstructed the classical problem of civic time and fortune as a counterweight to providential thinking, or who conducted a deliberate philosophical insurgency against Christian moral culture under the cover of rhetorical prudence. These readings are learned and serious. They have also, this book argues, systematically misread the epistemic environment that formed him.

What the standard readings of Machavelli identify as a break from the Christian tradition is more accurately understood as a diagnosis of it — conducted from the inside, using the tradition's own categories, by someone who understood its failures with the clarity that only intimate familiarity produces.

---

[61] Leo Strauss, *Thoughts on Machiavelli* (Glencoe, IL: Free Press, 1958), 9, 26, 334n72.

CHAPTER 5

Key Concepts Without Moral Theater

Chapter 3 showed what Machiavelli's central terms carried when they arrived to him: *virtù* saturated with Thomistic moral theology, *fortuna* freighted with a millennium of tension between contingency and providential order, *necessità* bounded by the natural law tradition, *gloria* shadowed by Augustine's extended critique. These were not neutral analytical instruments available for political use. They were Christian Latin concepts with deep institutional and theological histories, recognizable to every reader Machiavelli addressed.

This chapter examines what he did with them — how he redirected their weight from theological toward political analysis, and why that redirection is the move that makes him both unsettling and indispensable. He did not invent a new vocabulary. He turned the tradition's own language against the tradition's preferred consolations.

⁂

Machiavelli's political vocabulary resists easy alignment with modern moral categories. His central terms function as analytical instruments, not ethical ideals or objects of condemnation. He employs them to describe how political systems behave under pressure and how authority operates when circumstances constrain choice. Read in this way, these concepts belong to institutional mechanics, not moral provocation.[62]

This pattern reflects the environment in which Machiavelli wrote. In European Christendom, political language carried moral weight. Terms such as virtue, fortune, necessity, honor, and reputation structured sermons, legal reasoning, and public ritual. Political legitimacy was articulated through moral vocabulary, and moral failure often served as political explanation. Machiavelli works within this

[62] Skinner, *Foundations*, vol. 1, 130–168; Pocock, *Machiavellian Moment*, 156–218.

linguistic environment while redirecting its function. He repurposes inherited moral language to analyze political behavior.

The most central of these terms is *virtù*. Rather than moral quality, *virtù* names a capacity: the ability to act effectively within a given configuration of forces. It encompasses decisiveness, adaptability, foresight, and the capacity to impose order when disorder threatens. Under conditions of institutional strain, *virtù* may require actions that conflict with conventional moral expectations.[63] Its measure lies in effect, not intention.

Machiavelli evaluates political action by the durability of the order it produces. A ruler may act with mercy and still destroy a state through hesitation. Another may act harshly and stabilize authority. These outcomes are assessed through their political consequences. *Virtù* is revealed through sustained effect, never through declared motive.

Set alongside *virtù* is *fortuna*. Fortune names the element of contingency that pervades political life: war, plague, economic disruption, succession crises, and shifts in popular mood. Institutions can limit exposure to uncertainty, but they cannot remove it. Machiavelli's emphasis on *fortuna* underscores the limits of control and rejects the assumption that moral righteousness secures political success.[64]

The interaction between *virtù* and *fortuna* structures Machiavelli's analysis. Political skill consists in acting decisively where control is partial, anticipating instability, and preparing for reversal. Temporary success signals a momentary alignment of capacity and circumstance. Endurance depends on readiness, not mastery.

Closely related is necessity. Necessity names the constraints imposed by circumstance: limited resources, hostile rivals, internal division, and time pressure. Political actors choose within narrowing fields.[65] Effective judgment responds to constraint instead of disregarding it.

Machiavelli therefore evaluates rulers by outcomes produced under pressure. Declared motives function as political language — often sincere, sometimes

[63] Machiavelli, *The Prince*, chs. 6, 15, 18, 25; *Discourses*, I.2–6, III.1; Skinner, *Machiavelli*, 40–53.
[64] Machiavelli, *The Prince*, chap. 25; *Discourses*, I.1–2, III.1.
[65] Machiavelli, *The Prince*, chs. 6, 15, 18, 25; *Discourses*, I.1–4, III.1.

strategic — but they do not explain results. Decisions acquire meaning through their adequacy to the conditions that limit choice.

Reputation forms another central concept. Reputation operates as political capital. Rulers govern through law and force, but also through expectation. Subjects, allies, and rivals act on beliefs about what a ruler is capable of doing. Reputation shapes obedience, deterrence, and alliance by organizing those beliefs in advance.[66]

This explains Machiavelli's attention to appearances. In political life, appearance participates in reality. A ruler believed to be weak becomes weak through the actions of others.[67] A ruler believed to be decisive deters challenge even with limited means. Moral language, ritual display, and public conduct contribute to this process by conditioning expectation. They shape the effectiveness of force instead of replacing it.

Stability depends on alignment between appearance and capacity. Where that alignment holds, authority consolidates. Where it fractures, legitimacy erodes. Machiavelli treats this dynamic as structural, not deceptive. Political authority is mediated through perception, and neglecting that mediation produces predictable failure.

Underlying these concepts is Machiavelli's commitment to what he called the *effectual truth* of politics: how power operates in practice, not how it is imagined to operate.[68] Political theory loses explanatory force when it describes ideal arrangements unable to endure real conditions. Machiavelli's project proceeds diagnostically, tracing the mechanisms that allow institutions to survive pressure.

This posture governs his treatment of cruelty and mercy. He evaluates them as practices with consequences, not as moral absolutes. Limited and decisive severity can prevent prolonged disorder. Indulgence that allows instability to persist can produce greater harm over time. The analytic question concerns effect, not purity.

---

66 Machiavelli, *The Prince*, chs. 17–18, 21; Weber, *Economy and Society*.

67 Machiavelli, *The Prince*, chs. 17–19, 21.

68 Machiavelli, *The Prince*, ch. 15; Skinner, *Foundations*, 130–168.

The same logic applies to law and force. Law without enforcement functions as a declaration. Force without legitimacy remains unstable.[69] Political order emerges from their interaction. Institutions translate authority into compliance through norms, incentives, and sanctions. Where this translation fails, collapse follows.

What unifies Machiavelli's key concepts is their resistance to moral theater. Moral language plays an active role in political life by shaping legitimacy, mobilizing loyalty, and constraining action. It does not dissolve necessity, resolve conflict, or neutralize contingency. Political analysis that grants morality explanatory supremacy misreads how systems endure.

For readers formed within Christian moral traditions, this posture can feel unsettling. Machiavelli may appear to reduce politics to technique. His analysis instead relocates moral judgment. Evaluation shifts from intention to consequence, from profession to performance, from rhetoric to resilience. The central question concerns whether political arrangements can endure the conflicts they generate.

This distinction also sets limits on how Machiavelli's analysis should be used. Description does not confer endorsement, and diagnosis does not supply a playbook. Clarity identifies constraint without abolishing responsibility.

This is the discipline Machiavelli demands of his readers. He directs attention away from comforting abstractions and toward structure, pressure, and effect. The result is not cynicism, but clarity — and clarity is the first condition of any serious engagement with power.

---

[69] Weber, *Economy and Society*, 212–215.

PART II

The Architecture of Christendom

Part I established how Machiavelli was formed — the institutional origins of his Latin, his rhetorical training, his analytical vocabulary, and his political problems. Part II turns to the specific structural features of Christendom that his analysis was built to diagnose. This is not a general description of medieval civilization. It is an account of the architectural conditions that produced the failures he observed: the plural and permanently contested character of authority, the constitutional emergency that revealed what happened when the system's own adjudicative center collapsed, and the specific human beings that these conditions shaped and that governance had to manage.

Chapter 6 argues that the structural pluralism of authority in Christendom — the overlapping jurisdictions of pope, emperor, king, bishop, city, and guild, each holding enforceable claims backed by the same Christian moral vocabulary — was not a failure of the system but its designed condition. The Investiture Controversy established the dual-jurisdiction framework in the eleventh century; the centuries that followed filled it with an increasingly complex set of competing claimants. This is the world Machiavelli spent fourteen years navigating as a diplomat. His theory of authority — that it must be maintained rather than merely possessed, that legitimacy and capacity must reinforce one another or each collapses without the other — is a direct response to a specific structural reality, not a general observation about governance.

Chapter 7 shows the supreme instance of structural failure: the Western Schism, in which the institution specifically assigned to adjudicate among competing authorities lost the capacity to adjudicate itself. This was not a political embarrassment. It was a constitutional emergency — a moment when the civilization's court of last instance became itself the site of an authority dispute it could not resolve through its own mechanisms. The chapter traces the emergency response, the conciliarist solution, the papal consolidation that followed, and the institutional cost of that consolidation: a system restored to formal unity at the price of reduced capacity for self-correction. Machiavelli inherited that trade-off. His analytical sharpness about the gap between institutional claims and institutional capacity was formed in direct contact with its consequences.

Chapter 8 closes the part by examining the human material these structures produced and that political systems had to govern. Machiavelli's anthropology is often read as a general claim about human nature — pessimistic, universal, ahistorical. The revised chapter resists that reading. The people he analyzed were formed by Christian institutions, motivated partly by Christian moral language, operating within political frameworks organized through specifically Christian categories of legitimacy, obligation, and conscience. Formation of that kind was real and consequential. What Machiavelli insisted on — against the characteristic assumption of moralized political culture — was that it did not eliminate the underlying patterns: ambition, fear, the fragility of loyalty, the limits of gratitude. It gave them particular shapes. Reading those shapes clearly, without consolation, was the beginning of any political analysis worth having.

CHAPTER 6

Competing Authorities

In Machiavelli's world, the question of who held authority was never straightforward. It was never meant to be. Christendom had been built across centuries in a way that distributed authority among overlapping claimants, each with enforceable claims, each drawing on the same Christian moral vocabulary to justify demands that frequently contradicted one another. A Florentine merchant in the 1490s might find his marriage regulated by Church courts, his commercial disputes adjudicated by guild tribunals, his property claims subject to both canon and civil law, his military service owed to a republic whose legitimacy was contested by returned exiles, and his ultimate spiritual welfare governed by a papacy whose political conduct Machiavelli would shortly describe as one of the principal sources of Italy's ruin. Authority was not concentrated; it was distributed, layered, contested, and permanently unresolved.

This was not dysfunction — it was the designed condition of Christendom. Understanding why requires a brief account of how authority in Christian Europe became structurally plural — and what that plurality cost.

I. The Investiture Controversy and Its Long Shadow

The conflict that most sharply defined the structural problem of authority in Christendom began in 1076, when Pope Gregory VII excommunicated the Holy Roman Emperor Henry IV.[70] The immediate issue was the right to invest bishops — to appoint them to their offices and give them the symbols of their authority. But the underlying question was more fundamental: who held supreme authority in a Christian civilization? Was the emperor sovereign over the Church within his territories, as secular rulers had long assumed? Or did the pope, as the vicar of Christ, hold ultimate authority over all Christians including emperors, who were therefore subject to papal judgment in both spiritual and temporal affairs?

Henry's humiliation at Canossa in 1077 — standing barefoot in the snow for three days to seek the pope's absolution — became one of the most symbolically

[70] Blumenthal, *Investiture Controversy*, chaps. 4; Berman, *Law and Revolution*, 86.

charged moments in medieval political history.[71] It appeared to settle the question in Rome's favor. It settled nothing. Henry recovered his throne, resumed the conflict, and the contest between papal and imperial authority continued for generations. The Concordat of Worms in 1122 produced a compromise that distinguished spiritual investiture (the pope's prerogative) from temporal investiture (the emperor's), but the distinction was inherently unstable because bishops held both spiritual and temporal roles simultaneously. The boundary the Concordat drew could not hold where the two jurisdictions were fused in a single person exercising a single office.

The long-term consequence was the establishment of a principle that shaped European political life for the next four centuries: secular and ecclesiastical authority were distinct, each legitimate within its own sphere, and the boundary between those spheres was permanently contested.[72] Every subsequent conflict between pope and emperor, every dispute over clerical immunity from secular courts, every argument about the limits of papal taxation — all of these were replays of the Investiture Controversy in specific local contexts. Machiavelli was born into a civilization whose political architecture had been built on this unresolved tension.

II. The Landscape of Competing Claims

The Investiture Controversy established the framework. The centuries that followed filled it with an increasingly complex set of competing claimants, each contesting the boundaries of jurisdiction and each capable of backing its claims with real institutional force.

Papal authority over secular rulers extended well beyond the appointment of bishops. Popes claimed the right to release subjects from their oaths of allegiance to excommunicated rulers, effectively licensing rebellion.[73] They claimed jurisdiction over marriage and inheritance, which meant control over dynastic succession — the most consequential political question any medieval ruler faced. They claimed the power to adjudicate disputes between Christian princes and to call crusades that could redirect the military resources of multiple kingdoms

[71] Berman, *Law and Revolution*, 95-98.

[72] Kantorowicz, *King's Two Bodies*, 126; Strayer, *Medieval Origins*, 20-21.

[73] Tierney, *Crisis of Church and State*, 1–15.

simultaneously. The papacy was not merely a spiritual institution with occasional political interventions. It was a continuous political actor whose decisions shaped the practical options of every secular ruler in Europe.

Secular rulers responded by developing competing theories of royal authority. The doctrine of the divine right of kings, in its various medieval forms, insisted that monarchs received their authority directly from God, not through the mediation of the Church. French and English jurists developed arguments for the immunity of royal courts from papal jurisdiction. Imperial theorists argued that the emperor's authority was co-equal with the pope's in temporal matters and derived from a separate divine mandate. These were not merely theoretical positions. They were arguments deployed in active conflicts over taxation, legal jurisdiction, and the appointment of officials — arguments whose outcomes determined who held real power in specific territories.

Within kingdoms, the competition for authority extended further. Noble families claimed hereditary privileges that limited what kings could demand of their own subjects. Great lords maintained private armies, administered their own justice, collected their own revenues, and negotiated with the crown as near-equals in periods of royal weakness. The English barons who forced Magna Carta in 1215 were not anomalous. Across Europe, the consolidation of royal authority was a slow, contested, and repeatedly reversed process. Kingdoms were less unified political units than networks of negotiated relationships in which the king's authority was one claim among many.

Within the Church, authority was similarly fragmented. The conflict between papal centralization and episcopal independence ran throughout the medieval period.[74] Bishops claimed authority within their dioceses that was not merely delegated from Rome but derived from their own office as successors to the apostles. Cathedral chapters claimed rights against both bishops and popes. Religious orders operated under papal privileges that exempted them from episcopal jurisdiction. Mendicant friars could preach and hear confessions in parishes over the objection of local clergy. The Church was not a unified hierarchy with clear lines of command. It was an institution in which jurisdictional disputes were endemic and authority at every level was contested.

---

[74] Southern, *Western Society and the Church*, chaps. 3–4; Brundage, *Medieval Canon Law*, 70–75.

The conciliarist movement of the late fourteenth and early fifteenth centuries brought this internal fragmentation to a crisis.[75] The Western Schism — which this book examines in detail in the following chapter — produced a situation in which the papacy's claim to be Christianity's court of last instance collapsed entirely. The conciliarist response, developed by theologians and canon lawyers at Paris and Constance, argued that authority in the Church resided ultimately in a general council representing the whole Church, not in the pope alone. The Council of Constance resolved the Schism in 1417 by deposing rival claimants and electing a single pope — an act that required asserting council authority over the papacy itself.

The conciliarist episode had lasting consequences beyond its immediate resolution of the Schism. It demonstrated that the papacy's claim to supreme and unreviewable authority within the Church could be challenged on constitutional grounds using the Church's own legal and theological resources. The question of where final authority resided — in the pope alone, in pope together with council, or in the council when the pope failed — remained unresolved and explosively relevant throughout Machiavelli's lifetime. The Reformation that erupted in 1517, the year of Machiavelli's greatest diplomatic activity, was in part an aftershock of that unresolved constitutional question.

In Italy specifically, the competition of authorities took a distinctive form shaped by the peninsula's political fragmentation.[76] The Italian city-republics — Florence, Venice, Genoa, Siena, Lucca among them — had developed robust traditions of civic self-governance that competed directly with both imperial and papal claims to authority. Florentine jurists argued for the legal autonomy of the commune against external jurisdiction. Venetian practice systematically limited papal influence over ecclesiastical appointments within the republic's territory. These cities were not simply defying external authority. They had developed alternative theories of legitimate governance grounded in civic participation, legal tradition, and the common good — theories that coexisted uneasily with the universal claims of both papacy and empire.

Alongside the republics, the Italian signorie — lordships where a single family had consolidated power over a city and its surrounding territory — occupied a

[75] Tierney, *Foundations of Conciliar Theory*, 8–34, 195–220; Oakley, *Conciliarist Tradition*, ch. 1–3.
[76] Skinner, *Foundations*, vol. 1, 6-12; Najemy, *Italy in the Age of the Renaissance*, ch. 3.

different position in the authority landscape. The Sforza in Milan, the Este in Ferrara, the Gonzaga in Mantua had all risen through combinations of force, dynastic alliance, and the purchase or seizure of imperial or papal titles that gave their de facto power a veneer of legitimacy. Their authority was real and often effective, but its legal foundations were contested and its continuity depended on maintaining the right relationships with the larger powers — papacy, empire, France, Spain — whose endorsement could make or unmake a signore's claim.

This was the specific political environment Machiavelli spent fourteen years navigating as a Florentine official and diplomat. He was not observing competing authorities from a scholarly distance. He was managing them — negotiating with papal legates, assessing imperial intentions, calculating the reliability of French commitments, managing Florence's relationships with hostile neighbors and unreliable allies. The analysis of authority that appears in his writing is the product of direct engagement with a world in which authority was genuinely plural, permanently contested, and never finally resolved.

III. What Structural Contestation Produces

The authority landscape just described has a direct consequence for reading Machiavelli's theory of legitimacy. He was not developing a general account of how authority works in the abstract and illustrating it with historical examples. He was responding to a specific problem: how does authority function — how does it stabilize, sustain itself, and survive challenge — in a world where legitimacy is not settled but permanently contested?

In a world with a single unquestioned source of legitimate authority, the analytical questions are relatively limited: Does this ruler have the right credentials? Has the appropriate authority sanctioned his rule? Is he governing within established norms? Compliance follows from these answers. Resistance is deviance.

In Christendom, none of those questions had clean answers. Every major authority claim was contested by at least one competing authority with its own legitimate basis and its own enforcement capacity. A ruler could simultaneously hold valid title under one framework (imperial grant) while being excommunicated under another (papal sanction). A city's legal autonomy could be legally grounded in imperial privilege and simultaneously challenged by papal jurisdiction and noble hereditary claims. Subjects navigating these overlapping claims faced not a question of compliance with legitimate authority but a constant set of choices about which competing claim to honor and at what cost.

This is the world that produced Machiavelli's theory of authority — and understanding it transforms how that theory should be read. When he insists that authority must be maintained, not merely possessed, he is not stating an abstract truth about governance. He is describing a specific structural condition: in a world where multiple authorities compete for the same subjects, the authority that persists is the one that successfully organizes compliance, not the one with the best theoretical claim. When he argues that legitimacy and capacity must reinforce one another, he is observing that in Christendom they frequently did not — and that the gap between them was the specific vulnerability that foreign invasion, factional collapse, and institutional decay repeatedly exploited.

The analytical framework that follows is therefore best read as a diagnostic tool developed for a specific kind of political environment: one in which authority is structurally contested, moral language is simultaneously sincere and strategic, and the distance between what rulers claim and what they can actually enforce is the central political fact.

IV. Authority, Legitimacy, and the Analytical Framework

Authority is one of Machiavelli's central concerns and among the most frequently misread aspects of his work. In his account, authority is not synonymous with domination backed by force.[77] He draws a careful distinction between power that merely compels and authority that stabilizes. The difference lies in institutional structure and public recognition — and that distinction was forged in direct response to a world where both elements were in constant supply and constant competition.

Authority, as Machiavelli understands it, is relational. It exists only insofar as it is recognized.[78] A ruler may possess armies, wealth, and legal title yet fail to exercise authority if subjects, elites, or rivals withdraw acceptance of command.

[77] Machiavelli, *The Prince*, chs. 15–19; Weber, *Economy and Society*, 212–301.
[78] Machiavelli, *The Prince*, chap. 17.

Conversely, a ruler with limited resources may govern effectively when expectations align in his favor. Authority therefore functions as an ongoing condition, not a fixed possession. It must be maintained as circumstances change.

This emphasis explains Machiavelli's focus on legitimacy. Legitimacy refers to the shared understanding that a ruler's commands ought to be obeyed. In Christendom, that understanding was articulated through religious language, custom, law, and precedent.[79] Rulers appealed to divine sanction, inherited rights, and public service to justify their position. These appeals shaped compliance and resistance alike by organizing how authority was interpreted.

Legitimacy alone, however, does not sustain authority. Claims to rightful rule dissolve when they cannot be enforced. Authority requires capacity. Laws derive force from sanctions. Titles carry weight when they are backed by effective power. Enduring authority emerges when legitimacy and capacity reinforce one another.

Machiavelli is attentive to the danger of mistaking symbols of authority for its substance.[80] Ritual, ceremony, and moral language can sustain obedience when they correspond to real power. When appearances drift away from capacity, authority becomes brittle. States collapse because they continue to rely on moral language after the conditions that made it credible have eroded.

This problem takes on particular intensity in Christendom. Shared Christian moral language encouraged rulers to assume that belief could compensate for institutional weakness. Appeals to faith, unity, or divine favor were treated as substitutes for discipline, administration, and enforcement. Machiavelli treats this assumption as structurally dangerous. Moral consensus cannot arrest political decline. It can accelerate it by obscuring institutional failure.

Consistency is therefore central to authority. Machiavelli observes that arbitrary rule corrodes obedience. Predictable enforcement allows subjects to adjust behavior to stable expectations. Unpredictable punishment produces instability, tying authority to personal mood instead of law. Where rule becomes personal instead of institutional, intrigue and revolt multiply because no reliable framework for action exists.

---

[79] Tierney, *Crisis of Church and State*, 1–20.
[80] Machiavelli, *The Prince*, chs. 15–18.

For this reason, Machiavelli favors authority that operates impersonally where possible. Laws, offices, and procedures distribute responsibility and constrain caprice.[81] Even in principalities, where power is concentrated, regularized governance strengthens authority. Power grounded solely in personal charisma or terror proves fragile. Authority embedded in institutions survives succession, crisis, and error.

The relationship between authority and fear is among Machiavelli's most contested themes. His claim that it is safer for a ruler to be feared than loved,[82] when both cannot be secured, addresses reliability, not cruelty. Love depends on benefit and affection. Fear, when bounded and predictable, is tied to consequence. Authority anchored in predictable sanction holds more steadily than authority dependent on sentiment.

Calibration remains essential. Excessive or arbitrary fear generates hatred, which Machiavelli treats as politically dangerous because it motivates active opposition. Subjects who fear punishment without hatred tend toward compliance. Subjects who hate a ruler seek removal. Authority therefore requires deterrence without provoking resentment.

Reputation plays a central role in sustaining this balance. Authority strengthens when rulers are known to act decisively, enforce laws consistently, and respond effectively to threats. Reputation shapes expectations in advance, reducing the need for constant enforcement. Rivals hesitate, subjects comply, and allies commit. Reputation must remain grounded in actual capacity, however. A reputation for strength unsupported by reality invites challenge.

Machiavelli also emphasizes beginnings. Authority is easiest to establish at a regime's founding, when expectations are still forming. Early decisions signal the character of rule to come. Leniency at moments requiring firmness establishes precedents that prove difficult to reverse. Decisive action at the outset can stabilize authority even when later governance moderates. Timing shapes authority as much as intention.

---

81 Machiavelli, *The Prince*, chap. 17.

82 Machiavelli, *The Prince*, chs. 17, 19.

This sensitivity to timing reflects Machiavelli's view of political life as dynamic. Authority is sustained through adaptation and institutional maintenance; it is never secured once and for all. Rulers who mistake stability for permanence fail to prepare for change. When conditions shift, authority collapses because it was never reinforced structurally.

Machiavelli's account offers little consolation. Authority is presented as a human construction sustained by belief, enforcement, and institutional coherence.[83] When these elements drift apart, authority decays regardless of personal virtue. His realism lies in tracing the conditions under which authority can persist without illusion.

To understand authority in Machiavelli's sense is to recognize it as something built, maintained, and repaired. It depends on institutions that function under pressure, rulers attentive to limits, and populations whose expectations are shaped by consistent practice.

In Christendom, where authority was saturated with moral meaning and structurally contested at every level, these dynamics were especially difficult to acknowledge. Machiavelli forces them into view. Authority, in his account, is revealed not by what rulers claim, but by what endures when those claims are tested — against rivals with equally valid titles, against foreign armies with superior force, against subjects who have learned to read the gap between legitimacy and capacity with as much precision as their rulers.

---

[83] Machiavelli, *The Prince*, chs. 15–18; Berman, *Law and Revolution*, 1–44.

CHAPTER 7

Christianity Without a Center

Chapter 6 described a world of structurally competing authorities — papal and imperial, royal and episcopal, civic and noble — each drawing on the same Christian moral vocabulary to legitimate demands that frequently contradicted one another. That system of competing claims required, at minimum, one institution capable of serving as a court of last instance: a recognized terminus where escalating disputes could finally be resolved. Without such a terminus, the competition of authorities had no ceiling. Every conflict could, in principle, escalate indefinitely.

For much of the medieval period, the papacy supplied that terminus. It was contested, imperfectly enforced, and perpetually negotiated — but it was recognized.[84] When the system reached an impasse it could not resolve locally, there was a named place where judgment was supposed to end. The architectural importance of this function cannot be overstated. In a civilization built on competing claims, the institution that could credibly claim to adjudicate among them held a structural position that was irreplaceable.

In the late fourteenth century, that institution lost the capacity to perform its own function. The crisis that followed was not merely a political embarrassment or a spiritual scandal. It was a constitutional emergency — a moment when the system designed to resolve authority disputes became itself the site of an authority dispute it could not resolve. Machiavelli was born in 1469, within living memory of that emergency's resolution, into a civilization that had experienced the collapse of its own governing center and had not fully recovered from what that collapse revealed.

✦

For much of the Middle Ages, the papacy functioned as Christianity's court of last instance. Popes confirmed bishops, adjudicated disputes, granted exemptions, levied revenues, and claimed universal jurisdiction over the Western Church. Enforcement varied and was often contested, yet the office supplied something

[84] Tierney, *Foundations of Conciliar Theory*, 8–34.

indispensable: a recognized terminus for escalation. When disagreements exceeded local capacity, the system named where judgment was supposed to end.

In the late fourteenth century, that terminus failed.

Beginning in 1378, Western Christendom entered an unprecedented condition. Multiple men simultaneously claimed to be the legitimate pope.[85] Each had been elected by a body of cardinals. Each controlled territory. Each appointed bishops, issued decrees, collected revenues, and condemned rivals. Kings, cities, universities, monasteries, and clerical networks faced forced alignment decisions under conditions of uncertainty, with the expectation that later settlement might retroactively judge their choice.

The schism was a fracture at the top of the system. The institution assigned to provide final judgment became the site of division, and the system lacked a settled procedure for resolving division at that level. Consequences followed quickly. Obedience tracked political alliances. Clergy received ordinations later disputed. Legal judgments diverged. Appeals accumulated without a single authoritative path of review. The language of legitimacy continued, while the machinery that stabilized it lost coordinating force.

The destabilization came from more than rival claimants. It came from procedural indeterminacy: the system had to identify an authority capable of authoritatively identifying authority. Doctrine and law remained present, yet both relied on a functioning adjudicative center to interpret and apply them. Western Christianity entered what can be described, in institutional terms, as a constitutional emergency.

◆

The solution that took shape relocated authority upward and outward. If a single pope could not credibly perform executive finality, decisive governance required another forum. The general council emerged as that forum: an assembly claiming to represent the Church as a whole and empowered to act on its behalf when ordinary governance failed.

---

[85] Howard Kaminsky, "The Great Schism," in *The New Cambridge Medieval History*, vol. 6, c. 1300–c. 1415, ed. Michael Jones (Cambridge: Cambridge University Press, 2000), 674–96.

Councils had long existed, with roles in doctrine and crisis response. The innovation lay in the jurisdiction claimed for them under emergency conditions. Councils were asserted to possess authority to judge papal claimants and impose binding resolutions on the entire Church.[86] This was framed as a necessity response: when the executive center breaks, decisions must be reconstituted at a higher level to preserve unity and continuity. The council became a temporary locus of authority designed to restore coherence when ordinary channels could not.

The Council of Constance embodied this logic. Convened to resolve the schism, it asserted jurisdiction over all Western Christians — including papal claimants — on the grounds that paralysis threatened the institution's integrity.[87] It deposed rival popes, accepted resignations, and oversaw the election of a single recognized pontiff. The schism ended through imposed settlement: a forum capable of decisive action supplied the coordination mechanism the system required.

The settlement solved one crisis and opened another. Once a council claimed authority over popes under emergency conditions, the system faced a downstream constitutional question: what, exactly, bounded that authority after emergency conditions receded? If a representative assembly could govern the Church in extremis, the principle of that capacity could not easily be treated as a one-time exception. The emergency arrangement raised the question of control over escalation.

The dispute that followed centered on governance mechanics. Who could convene a council? Who set its agenda? Who confirmed its decisions? Who enforced its judgments?[88] These questions appeared in theological language, yet their substance was jurisdictional and procedural: where final authority resided when the system came under stress.

Advocates of conciliar authority argued that councils possessed inherent power derived from Christ and therefore could act without papal authorization.[89] Defenders of papal primacy argued that councils required papal convocation and

---

[86] Oakley, *Conciliarist Tradition*, chaps. 1–3.

[87] Tanner, *Decrees of the Ecumenical Councils*, vol. I, 409–451.

[88] Tierney, *Foundations of Conciliar Theory*, 195–220.

[89] Tierney, *Foundations of Conciliar Theory*, 222–256.

confirmation to exercise binding jurisdiction. The argument concerned sovereignty inside the institution: whether the executive office or representative assembly possessed final authority during the crisis and in its aftermath.

Some efforts sought to formalize the emergency arrangement. Proposals for regular councils would have transformed a crisis mechanism into a standing feature of Church governance. Such a structure would have embedded oversight into the system and made correction routine rather than exceptional.

A restored papacy treated this prospect as a threat to singular executive finality. Regular councils implied permanent competition at the top of the hierarchy. Authority would flow through a mixed constitution rather than a single center, and governance would oscillate between office and assembly.

The papal response therefore subordinated the conciliar form. Councils remained legitimate in principle, while their operational conditions tightened in practice.[90] Councils could convene, but through papal summons. They could deliberate, but within limits structured by papal authority. They could assist governance, while their capacity to override it was restricted to extreme edge cases.

Legal and doctrinal measures reinforced this settlement. Appeals from papal decisions to future councils were prohibited, closing a bypass channel.[91] The hierarchy of authority was clarified: outside rare cases tied to manifest heresy, the pope stood as the final judge. Emergency authority remained part of the historical memory and was neutralized as a standing governance option.

By the mid-fifteenth century, when Machiavelli entered the world, the acute crisis had passed. A single pope again stood at the head of Western Christianity. The consolidation carried an institutional cost: a reduced capacity for system-wide self-correction at speed.

Reform continued, largely downstream. Monastic orders renewed themselves. Individual bishops pursued pastoral reform.[92] New movements emphasized

[90] Oakley, *Conciliarist Tradition*, chaps. 4–6.
[91] Tierney, *Foundations of Conciliar Theory*, 250–256.
[92] O'Malley, *Trent*, 1–30.

discipline, education, and moral rigor. Some later took durable institutional form, combining intensive formation with strict obedience to strengthen the Church from within existing structures. These efforts operated within a system whose incentive flows and authority structure remained largely stable.

The result was accumulating strain. Moral expectations intensified while governance mechanisms remained centralized and slow. Appeals to conscience multiplied without equivalent growth in institutional responsiveness. In regions distant from Rome — particularly in northern Europe — the gap between authority's demands and its credibility widened.

When new challenges emerged in the early sixteenth century, rapid, legitimate, system-wide response proved difficult. Councils carried constitutional risk; papal control concerns slowed convocation; executive decree struggled to match problems that exceeded the reach of unilateral command.

The Council of Trent eventually met under necessity: a delayed, carefully managed reactivation of the conciliar form, stripped of constitutional ambition and firmly subordinated to papal authority.[93] The Church reformed while keeping the question of final governance location closed.

This was the institutional world Machiavelli inherited: a Christianity that endured a collapse of final authority, restored unity through emergency relocation, then tightened the channels that made such relocation possible. Unity returned; adaptability narrowed. Authority became singular again, with the memory of its failure still near.

It is this pattern — center fracture, emergency relocation, settlement through decisive action, consolidation through channel-control, and deferred costs — that Machiavelli later recognizes with unusual clarity: as a student of how institutions behave when legitimacy fractures and necessity forces choices meant for survival rather than permanence.[94]

---

[93] O'Malley, *Trent*, 50–95.

[94] Machiavelli, *Discourses*, I.18; Skinner, *Foundations*, vol. 1, 113–160.

CHAPTER 8

The Human Material of Politics

The preceding chapters have described Christendom's political architecture: the competing authorities, the contested jurisdictions, the constitutional crisis produced when the system's own adjudicative center failed. What animated that architecture, what moved through its channels and strained its structures, was human beings — ambitious, fearful, loyal under some conditions and treacherous under others, responsive to incentive and formation in ways that were patterned but never fully predictable.

This is Machiavelli's starting point, and it requires emphasis in the context just established. The people he observed and analyzed were not generic political actors operating in an abstract institutional environment. They were men and women formed by Christian institutions — educated in Church-affiliated schools, habituated by Christian ritual, motivated partly by Christian moral language, and operating within political frameworks that organized their ambitions and fears through specifically Christian categories of legitimacy, obligation, and sin. That formation was real and consequential. It shaped what they wanted, what they feared, and what justifications they reached for when competing for power. But Machiavelli's central analytical insight was that formation of this kind does not eliminate the underlying patterns of human behavior. It gives them particular shapes. Beneath the Christian moral vocabulary, the recurring patterns he had spent a career observing — ambition, fear, factional loyalty, the fragility of gratitude — operated with the same structural regularity they had exhibited in the Rome he read about and the Florence he served.

This focus distinguishes Machiavelli from both classical political philosophy and much Christian moral reflection. Classical writers often framed political order as an extension of reason,[95] with disorder attributed to ignorance or passion. Christian moral traditions have frequently interpreted political failure through

[95] Aristotle, *Politics*, I.1–2, III.6–7; Berlin, "*Originality of Machiavelli.*".

the language of sin, pride, or vice. Machiavelli shifts the analytic center. Human beings generate recurring patterns of behavior regardless of the moral language that surrounds them, and political analysis must begin with those patterns.

Ambition stands among the most persistent of these patterns. Individuals seek advantage, security, honor, and influence.[96] Elites compete for office and prestige, while popular groups resist domination and seek protection from exploitation. These impulses persist under moral exhortation. They can be redirected, restrained, or institutionalized, but they remain present. Political systems that assume their disappearance invite instability.

Fear operates with similar regularity across political life. Rulers fear the loss of power; elites fear displacement; populations fear disorder, punishment, and deprivation.[97] Machiavelli treats fear as a force whose effects depend on how it is organized. Diffuse or arbitrary fear produces resentment and revolt. Predictable and bounded fear sustains obedience. Authority depends on neither affection alone nor unstructured terror, but on disciplined management of consequence.

Loyalty exhibits comparable fragility. People remain loyal when loyalty aligns with interest, security, or expectation.[98] When conditions shift, professions of devotion erode. This reflects the contingent nature of political relationships, not a moral deficiency. Gratitude fades under pressure. Promises weaken when survival is at stake. Appeals to past service carry limited weight in moments of danger.

This observation functions as a warning against misplaced trust, not a declaration of cynicism. Machiavelli directs attention away from sentiment and toward structure. Political systems must function even when loyalty weakens, because reliance on unreliable attachments exposes authority to sudden collapse.

Faction forms another durable feature of political life. Inequality, status competition, and divergent interests generate organized conflict.[99] Machiavelli treats faction as an expression of underlying divisions, never as an anomaly. Systems that attempt total suppression tend to drive rivalry underground, where

---

96 Machiavelli, *Discourses*, bk. 1, chaps. 4–6, 37.

97 Machiavelli, *The Prince*, chs. 17, 19.

98 Machiavelli, *The Prince*, chs. 17–18.

99 Machiavelli, *Discourses*, bk. 1, chs. 4–7, 34; Pocock, *Machiavellian Moment*, 203–213.

it becomes conspiratorial and violent. More stable arrangements provide visible channels through which competition can unfold without destroying the polity.

Institutional design therefore occupies a central place in Machiavelli's analysis. When ambition and resentment lack lawful outlets, pressure accumulates until rupture occurs. Institutions that permit rivalry — through offices, assemblies, courts, and procedures — convert destructive energy into manageable competition. Stability arises from structured disagreement, not from consensus.

Gratitude, often praised as a civic virtue, receives an unsentimental treatment. Benefits are remembered briefly, especially when they impose obligations.[100] Dependence more often breeds resentment than loyalty. Acts of generosity can reinforce authority when they are rare and visible. When they become routine, they lose force. Political systems that rely on gratitude as a durable foundation misread human memory.

Underlying these observations is Machiavelli's assessment of the pace at which human behavior changes. Education, religion, and culture shape conduct gradually and unevenly, while political crises unfold rapidly. Rulers act with the material available to them, not with an imagined citizenry produced by ideal formation. Political systems frequently fail because they are designed for people who do not yet exist.

Machiavelli is attentive to human inconsistency. Individuals exhibit courage and cowardice, generosity and envy, discipline and indulgence — often in close succession.[101] Political theory that assumes stable character traits misreads this variability. Machiavelli acknowledges virtue while treating its reliability as uncertain. Institutions therefore must absorb fluctuation; they cannot depend on moral steadiness.

This perspective informs his account of popular opinion. Populations respond to visible outcomes, credible signals, and immediate conditions. They can be misled temporarily, but sustained misrule generates resistance regardless of rhetoric. Opinion shifts with experience, not instruction.

---

[100] Machiavelli, *The Prince*, chap. 17.

[101] Machiavelli, *The Prince*, chs. 17–18.

Governance, in Machiavelli's account, aligns incentives with these human realities. Laws anticipate evasion. Offices assume competition.[102] Enforcement accounts for resistance. Moral language operates within the system as one force among others; it is no substitute for structure. When political design ignores human behavior, moral aspiration becomes a liability, not a resource.

This analysis does not reduce politics to psychology. Human behavior matters because it interacts with institutions. Ambition expressed through lawful competition differs from ambition expressed through conspiracy. Fear channeled through predictable sanction differs from fear produced by arbitrary violence. Identical impulses generate different outcomes depending on the systems that organize them.

Many political failures arise from confusing moral description with operational reality.[103] Rulers describe subjects as faithful, grateful, or obedient, and then govern as though those descriptions were stable conditions. When circumstances shift, the descriptions collapse and authority follows. Machiavelli insists on separating how people are spoken about from how they behave when incentives change.

To study the human material of politics, then, is to adopt a disciplined view of humanity, not a bleak one. Political systems cannot rely on virtue as a constant.[104] Stability depends on institutions that function when virtue falters, loyalty weakens, and fear intrudes.

❖

This insight forms the foundation of Machiavelli's realism. Before legitimacy is secured, before authority is justified, and before power is exercised with restraint, governance must confront the material it governs. Human beings are volatile, adaptive, and responsive to pressure. Political wisdom begins by acknowledging what that material actually is — and designing institutions capable of functioning with it, not against it.[105]

---

[102] Machiavelli, *Discourses*, bk. 1, chs. 3, 7, 18; *The Prince*, chs. 15, 18–19.
[103] Skinner, *Foundations*, 150–160; Berlin, "*Originality of Machiavelli*," 36–52.
[104] Machiavelli, *The Prince*, chs. 15, 17–18, 25; *Discourses*, bk. 1, chs. 3, 18, 58.
[105] Machiavelli, *The Prince*, chs. 15, 17–18, 25; *Discourses*, bk. 1, chs. 3, 4, 39.

PART III
The Machinery of Rule

Part II described Christendom's architecture under stress: the structural pluralism of competing authorities, the constitutional emergency when the adjudicative center collapsed, and the specific human material those conditions produced. Part III turns from the architecture to the machinery — how authority is actually exercised, preserved, and scaled in a world where jurisdiction is contested, legitimacy is moralized, and conflict is normal. Machiavelli's analytical contribution here is methodological: he treats power as institutional, not personal; structured, not spontaneous; transmitted through design, not through character. He describes what the machinery does, not what it claims to do — which means, in Christendom specifically, describing what the machinery does when moral language and institutional capacity pull apart.

The five chapters examine five interlocking elements. Chapter 9 examines office and the burden of command: how the person/office distinction that Christendom developed over centuries functioned as a continuity mechanism, and why governing through moralized office created collision between goods as a structural condition, not an exceptional one. Chapter 10 examines executive power and necessity: how crisis compresses decision-making into forced moves, why *necessità* was not an abstract concept but the permanent operating condition of a civilization that could not resolve the question of supreme jurisdiction. Chapter 11 examines indirect rule: how authority becomes continuous through intermediaries, offices, and procedure, and why the most elaborate infrastructure of indirect rule in Christendom was ecclesiastical, not secular. Chapter 12 examines reputation and public credibility: how authority operates upstream of enforcement through the management of belief, and why Christendom's moralized legitimacy made reputation simultaneously more powerful and more fragile than in less moralizing political systems. Chapter 13 examines faction and institutional design: conflict as a permanent condition requiring institutional organization, and why the moralization of political conflict in Christendom made this design problem systematically harder to acknowledge.

Together these five mechanisms constitute the operating logic of governance in a moralized civilization — the machinery that allowed Christendom's institutions to function under the conditions Parts I and II described. Identifying them in Machiavelli's analysis is only the first step. The larger claim, argued across the rest of the book, is that these mechanisms did not disappear when Christendom's theological unity fractured. They migrated. The office, the emergency power, the intermediary structure, the reputation system, the faction-processing institution — all of these appear in modern governance with different labels and different justificatory vocabularies, doing work that is recognizably continuous with what they did when the Church built and maintained them. That continuity is what makes Machiavelli indispensable not as a historical figure but as a diagnostic instrument for reading institutions that are still, in the most important structural sense, living inside the world he described.

CHAPTER 9

Office, Mandate, and the Burden of Command

In European Christendom, rule was publicly understood as an office of stewardship—a charge held under moral claims, articulated in Christian language, and measured by obligations that exceeded personal preference.[106] This made legitimacy "thick." Authority was a matter of duty-bearing office, publicly installed and publicly judged, as much as it was command or succession. Governance therefore tended to involve recurring collisions between goods, never clean moral choices. The office concentrated incompatible responsibilities and demanded decisions under conditions where every available option carried moral cost.

To understand political life in Christendom, one must distinguish the person from the office.[107] The person is fallible, replaceable, and morally mixed. The office functions as a continuity mechanism. It binds a community across time through succession, regency, title, and jurisdiction. Authority is anchored in a role already intelligible to subjects, intermediaries, and rivals, not from resting on personal charisma or private virtue.

This distinction helps explain why political order could persist through weak reigns, minority kingships, and periods of regency.[108] When the person became incapable, the office still governed in the name of the crown, the city, the realm, or the Church. Law, taxation, and command belonged to the office even when the occupant was absent, contested, or incompetent. Responsibility could be carried institutionally without resting entirely on the ruler's character or capacity.

The same distinction also structured resistance. Opposition could be framed as fidelity to the true office against a compromised occupant.[109] Factions claimed to defend the realm against a tyrant, to restore lawful order against a usurper, or to

[106] Kantorowicz, *The King's Two Bodies*, 3–23.
[107] Kantorowicz, *The King's Two Bodies*, 273–312.
[108] Strayer, *Medieval Origins*, 9–60.
[109] Tierney, *Crisis of Church and State*, 1–20.

protect the Church against an unworthy ruler. Even when such claims concealed interest, their form matters. The office supplied the grammar through which loyalty and dissent became intelligible within a moralized political world.

This clarifies what stability means in a fragmented order. Stability consists in the continued credibility of offices—royal, republican, ecclesial—such that obedience remains coordinated even under strain. Where the office retains credibility, institutions can absorb weakness in the occupant without immediate collapse. Where the office loses credibility, rule becomes personal and therefore brittle, dependent on continual reinforcement through force, bargaining, or fear.

Within this office-centered world, claims of divine mandate functioned primarily as a public grammar of legitimacy.[110] A ruler's inner piety mattered theologically, but the political mechanism operated through publicly legible forms. Phrases such as "by the grace of God" named the claimed source of authority, marked its limits, and implied obligations others could cite. Authority appeared as received, not invented; inherited, not improvised; and answerable to standards beyond convenience.

Because this grammar operated publicly, it remained effective even when sincerity was mixed. Legitimacy depends more on recognizability than on interior conviction.[111] Stewardship language bound rulers by creating standards others could invoke, enforce, and use to judge them. Moral language here functions structurally: it organizes public meaning, shapes reputational cost, and supplies categories through which both obedience and resistance are justified.

This is also why Machiavelli reads moral language as infrastructure, not ornament.[112] In Christendom specifically, where the grammar of stewardship descended from ecclesiastical investiture and where the same Latin vocabulary of office was used by bishops, kings, and city magistrates alike, this management of the moral register was not a peripheral concern — it was the primary medium through which competing claims to the same territory and population were fought and adjudicated.

[110] Kantorowicz, *The King's Two Bodies*, 3–23.

[111] Weber, *Economy and Society*, 212–217.

[112] Machiavelli, *The Prince*, chs. 15–18; Skinner, *Machiavelli*, 40–85.

If the mandate supplied the grammar of legitimacy, authorization mechanisms supplied its installation. In Christendom, legitimacy had to be made public. Coronations, anointings, oaths, acclamations, and juridical confirmations were procedures through which office became real to those whose recognition mattered.[113] These acts converted a private person into a public office-holder and coordinated expectations between ruler and ruled.

This logic also explains why rival claimants imitated the same forms. Political conflict was fought through competing installations of legitimacy: rival coronations, contested titles, alternative oaths, and fractured recognitions by key intermediaries. Anti-kings did more than seize power; they staged office.[114] Such imitation shows that the legitimacy system itself functioned as an arena in which political claims became credible—or failed.

Within this framework, elite obligation operated as a genuine constraint, not a mere social ideal.[115] To occupy rank or office was to accept publicly legible duties: protection of dependents, restraint in the use of power, willingness to bear risk, and administration of justice within one's jurisdiction. Privilege required justification through service. Obligation helped make authority credible.

Honor, in this setting, operated as an enforceable expectation.[116] Failure to meet obligation carried costs: withdrawal of elite cooperation, clerical resistance, loss of fiscal assent, or erosion of loyalty. A ruler who repeatedly deflected burdens downward or avoided risk might survive for a time, but he eroded the trust conditions that allowed governance without constant coercion.

The central claim of the chapter follows from this. When authority is understood as moralized office and obligation is publicly legible, governance becomes a site of collision between goods. The office concentrates responsibility precisely where responsibility is hardest.[117]

Mercy and deterrence pull in opposite directions. Unity and justice collide when enforcing law against powerful factions threatens a fragile polity.[118] Peace

[113] Kantorowicz, The King's Two Bodies, 46–87.
[114] Tierney, *The Crisis of Church and State*, 1050–1300, 1–20.
[115] Strayer, *On the Medieval Origins of the Modern State*, 35–60.
[116] Strayer, *On the Medieval Origins of the Modern State*, 35–60.
[117] Kantorowicz, *The King's Two Bodies*, 3–23.
[118] Kantorowicz, *The King's Two Bodies*, 3–23.

and defense conflict when avoiding war invites future invasion, yet waging war imposes immediate suffering. Truth and stability diverge when transparency risks panic or exploitation, yet concealment corrodes trust. Local loyalties and universal claims compete when rulers must choose between honoring particular obligations and sustaining broader order.

These tensions are structural features of rule in a moralized civilization. Each good is intelligible, publicly valued, and morally defensible. Circumstances force choice, and choice sacrifices one good for the sake of another. The office does not allow withdrawal from this responsibility. To hold office is to stand at the intersection of incompatible claims and decide which loss will be borne.

Tragic choice is best understood clinically, not theatrically. It names a governance condition in which every available action carries moral cost, and in which refusal to choose becomes its own consequential choice. The burden of command arises from the structure of the office itself. Machiavelli's realism begins here: political life repeatedly forces decisions between goods that cannot be harmonized under pressure.

The moralization of office cuts both ways. It constrains rulers by attaching obligations and raising the cost of abuse or neglect. It also enables rulers by furnishing a language through which difficult actions can be justified and coordinated.[119] Stewardship language limits legitimate action while rendering extraordinary measures intelligible as fulfillment of duty, not personal ambition.

This dual function explains why Christian moral vocabulary does real institutional work. It shapes incentives, expectations, and interpretation.[120] Machiavelli's attention to appearances, reputation, and public judgment reflects this reality. Moral language constrains and enables action at once, and it matters because it organizes what authority can plausibly do.

When legitimacy fractures in Christendom, failure tends to appear at the level of office. Contested succession produces rival claimants competing through titles, rituals, and recognition.[121] Jurisdictional overlap creates zones of ambiguity where

[119] Kantorowicz, *The King's Two Bodies*, 273–312.
[120] Harold J. Berman, *Law and Revolution: The Formation of the Western Legal Tradition* (Cambridge, MA: Harvard University Press, 1983), 85–164.
[121] Tierney, *The Crisis of Church and State*, 1050–1300, 1–20.

obedience becomes selective. Scandal and sacrilege delegitimate office even when coercive capacity remains. Persistent mismatch between claim and capacity erodes belief in the office itself, forcing coercion to work harder for diminishing returns.

These are predictable failure modes of a system in which authority is moralized, layered, and publicly enacted. Machiavelli's contribution lies in making these patterns visible without reducing them to individual vice.[122]

This chapter has described the moral frame within which rule operated in European Christendom: office as stewardship, mandate as legitimacy grammar, and command as the site where incompatible goods collide. This frame does not resolve the problem of governance; it explains why the problem takes the form it does.

What remains is to examine what happens when time collapses—when pressure intensifies, delay becomes dangerous, and decisions can no longer be deferred without loss.[123] Under these conditions, tragic collisions convert into forced moves, and authority concentrates around those capable of acting.

Machiavelli names this condition necessity. Necessity describes the pressure that reshapes political judgment when survival is at stake. The next chapter turns to that condition directly, tracing how executive power emerges and operates once the burden of command meets the scarcity of time.

---

[122] Machiavelli, *Discourses on Livy*, I.2; Skinner, *Machiavelli*, 40–85.

[123] Machiavelli, *The Prince*, chap. 25.

CHAPTER 10

Executive Power and Necessity

In Machiavelli's world, political decisions unfold under compression: invasion, revolt, fiscal strain, famine, disease, faction, and the persistent risk that institutions fail faster than they can respond.[124] What appears in retrospect as a sequence of policy choices is experienced in real time as a narrowing corridor of options in which delay becomes consequential.[125]

Under these conditions, politics shifts from debating ideals to preventing irreversible loss. Time contracts. Information arrives late or unevenly. Rivals exploit hesitation. Problems that could have been handled with limited measures in ordinary time compound into crisis because they were left pliable too long.

Executive power emerges at precisely this point. It begins as a practical response to a governance problem: when events move faster than collective deliberation can coordinate, decision and action must be unified. As delay turns into loss, authority concentrates.

Machiavelli names the condition producing this concentration necessity.[126] Necessity precedes choice. It describes the environment in which choice must be made: time scarcity, fractured information, and approaching irreversibility.

Invasion, rebellion, famine, and fiscal collapse impose urgency regardless of preference. The aim here is diagnostic: to identify the pressures that reshape judgment once ideal conditions vanish, and to clarify how governance changes when survival becomes the constraint.

Most political and legal institutions are built for ordinary time—relative continuity in which procedures, deliberation, and distributed authority function as intended. Ordinary time assumes decisions can be sequenced, information gathered, interests negotiated, and delay tolerated.

---

[124] Niccolò Machiavelli, *The Prince*, trans. Harvey C. Mansfield (Chicago: University of Chicago Press, 1998), chs. 3, 12; Niccolò Machiavelli, *Discourses on Livy*, trans. Harvey C. Mansfield and Nathan Tarcov (Chicago: University of Chicago Press, 1996), I.preface, I.2, I.34.

[125] Machiavelli, *The Prince*, chs. 3, 25.

[126] Machiavelli, *The Prince*, ch. 25; Machiavelli, *Discourses on Livy*, I.2.

Necessity names extraordinary times, when those assumptions fail. Procedures strain because the conditions that make them workable disappear. Deliberation becomes slower than events. Consultation increases leakage. Consensus becomes unattainable within the window available. Authority diffuses precisely when coherence becomes non-negotiable.[127]

Under such pressure, political systems often survive by improvising mechanisms they would not accept as permanent arrangements. The question necessity forces is whether a system can respond at all without dissolving. A polity may have excellent norms for ordinary time and still prove brittle under shock. Another may preserve itself in extraordinary time by suspending preferred forms long enough to avoid collapse.

Necessity compresses coordination as well as time. In ordinary conditions, governance can tolerate friction: committees, councils, layered consultation, distributed responsibility. Under a crisis, that friction becomes a liability. Misalignment grows costly, and the window for effective action narrows.

Executive authority concentrates as a response to this coordination problem. Concentration reduces decision points, simplifies command, and enables unified action. It creates a locus of responsibility when responsibility cannot safely be dispersed. The executive functions here as the mechanism that converts urgency into action before circumstances foreclose remaining options.

This is why executive concentration recurs across regimes with very different constitutional commitments.[128] Republics, monarchies, city-states, and empires repeatedly discover under pressure that someone must be able to decide and act. Emergency magistracies, delegated commands, extraordinary councils, temporary suspensions of procedure—these arise less from ideology than from time scarcity and the need for coordination.

Machiavelli treats this concentration without romance. Authority gathered under crisis can persist beyond the crisis that produced it. Systems that refuse to name necessity rarely avoid executive power; they invite it to reappear informally—through commanders acting without oversight, factions coordinating off-record, or actors exercising power without accountability.

---

[127] Machiavelli, *Discourses on Livy*, I.34.

[128] Machiavelli, *Discourses on Livy*, I.34.

Within necessity, Machiavelli treats decisiveness as a political capacity: clarity under constraint. Under crisis, indecision can be fatal to the polity the ruler is charged to preserve. Decisiveness means recognizing when delay compounds the threat and when partial measures no longer suffice.[129] Timing becomes an element of governance rather than an external inconvenience.

Delay frequently produces the severity later lamented.[130] Threats intensify. Opportunities narrow. What could have been handled with limited action becomes unmanageable, and the eventual response becomes harsher precisely because it was postponed. In ordinary conditions, caution can preserve stability; under necessity, caution can become functional abdication.

Necessity also clarifies the ruler's position inside constraint. Rulers govern as navigators. They inherit obligations they did not choose—treaties, debts, alliances, enmities, legal structures, traditions, expectations—and these delimit what can be done without breaking the system entirely.[131]

From the outside, executive power can look like freedom. From the inside, it often feels like a corridor of constrained moves. A ruler may wish to act generously with an exhausted treasury. He may prefer peace inside a strategic environment that makes peace fragile. He may want procedural regularity while rivals exploit delay. These constraints are the field within which responsibility is exercised.

This is why Machiavelli refuses to treat political outcomes as simple expressions of personal virtue or vice. Intent matters, but results depend on how well actions fit constraints that cannot be removed. Political skill includes distinguishing what can be bent from what must be endured, and acting before circumstances harden into irreversibility.

Necessity rearranges moral calculation by sequence. Under ordinary conditions, rulers may attempt to balance several goods at once—fairness, mercy, procedure, restraint. Under existential threat, those goods remain, but survival becomes the precondition under which other goods can continue to be pursued.[132]

---

129 Machiavelli, *The Prince*, ch. 3.

130 Machiavelli, *The Prince*, ch. 7.

131 Machiavelli, *The Prince*, ch. 25; Machiavelli, *Discourses on Livy*, I.2.

132 Machiavelli, *The Prince*, chs. 15, 18, 25.

This is why necessity feels morally abrasive. It forces survival into the foreground. A polity that collapses cannot sustain law, administer justice, defend the weak, or preserve civic and religious life. Under pressure, rulers face decisions in which every available option carries moral cost.

Governance under necessity becomes a choice between lesser disasters. The executive chooses among outcomes that each include injury—to lives, to justice, to trust, to stability, to the moral credibility of office.[133] Judgment consists in deciding which injury can be contained and which becomes catastrophic if avoided.

Because necessity compresses time and coordination, crisis repeatedly generates extraordinary powers and exceptional offices. Even regimes committed to distributed authority create special commissions, delegated commands, procedural suspensions, and extraordinary fiscal measures. Emergency power appears as a recurring response to a recurring condition, and systems that refuse to reckon with it often produce uncontrolled authority in less visible forms.

The central institutional risk is persistence. Extraordinary authority that goes unnamed resists bounds.[134] When it remains unbounded, crisis becomes an excuse rather than condition, and the exceptional becomes normal. Machiavelli holds this danger in view without consolation.

If necessity forces concentration, the central institutional problem becomes containment. Systems that contain emergency power tend to do two things: they name extraordinary conditions as extraordinary, and they define scope, duration, and accountability even while concentrating authority for action.[135] They also build a restoration pathway—the deliberate return of authority to ordinary institutions when pressure recedes. Without restoration, emergency measures harden into habit, and habit becomes structured.

Machiavelli implies this tension even when he does not formalize it as constitutional theory.[136] Crisis can be navigated; it can also be exploited.

---

[133] Machiavelli, *The Prince*, ch. 17.

[134] Machiavelli, *Discourses on Livy*, I.34.

[135] Machiavelli, *Discourses on Livy*, I.34.

[136] Machiavelli, *Discourses on Livy*, I.2; Skinner, *Machiavelli*, 40–85.

Extraordinary measures can preserve a state; they can also transform it. His diagnostic contribution is to hold both possibilities together.

This chapter has described a mechanism rather than an ideal. Pressure produces compression. Compression produces concentration. Concentration produces decisions with irreversible consequences. That chain is the effectual truth of governance under threat.[137] That this chain recurred so relentlessly in Christendom — a civilization that could not resolve the question of supreme jurisdiction and therefore guaranteed that any serious crisis would involve competing authorities each claiming emergency powers simultaneously — explains why Machiavelli treats necessity not as an exception to political life but as one of its permanent structural features.

With this mechanism in view, the chapters that follow can be read more precisely. Indirect rule, reputation, faction, and institutional design are attempts to stabilize authority so political communities avoid governing perpetually in emergency mode.[138] Where legitimacy is maintained and intermediaries cooperate, a polity can absorb shock without immediately concentrating power into naked coercion. Where these stabilizers fail, necessity becomes chronic and executive authority becomes harder to contain.

Machiavelli's realism begins in crisis and extends to the quieter problem that follows: building and preserving institutions capable of reducing the frequency with which necessity becomes the governing condition.

---

[137] Machiavelli, *The Prince*, ch. 15.

[138] Machiavelli, *Discourses on Livy*, I.2.

CHAPTER 11

Indirect Rule

Political power rarely operates through constant command. In complex societies, rulers govern by building systems that carry decisions forward without continuous personal involvement. This is the deeper structure of authority Machiavelli makes visible: indirect rule.

Indirect rule arises from scale. As political communities expand in territory, population, and institutional density, direct governance becomes impracticable.[139] A ruler cannot hear every case, judge every dispute, enforce every law, and administer every resource. Authority must be translated into structure.

Indirect rule is the art of governing through intermediaries. Offices, courts, councils, magistrates, ministers, guilds, and administrative bodies translate sovereign authority into daily practice. They create distance between ruler and ruled, allowing power to appear orderly, stable, and impersonal. Authority becomes embedded in routine, not spectacle.

Distance is a condition of durability. Authority that depends on constant personal intervention exhausts itself. It becomes reactive and brittle, tied to the ruler's physical presence and stamina. Authority that operates through institutions endures because it is carried by roles, procedures, and expectations.

Machiavelli treats insulation as a requirement of longevity. The ruler governs by designing structures that act reliably in his absence. As systems mature, the ruler can recede from view without losing effectiveness. Power is exercised continuously through offices even when the sovereign is unseen.

Indirect rule performs several essential functions. First, it multiplies power. A network of officials extends authority across geography and circumstance, enabling decisions to be made simultaneously in many places. Power scales through replication: each official becomes a node through which authority flows. Directives are interpreted, adapted, and applied. Variation enters through this translation, and governance becomes possible through it.

---

[139] Strayer, *Medieval Origins*, 35–60.

Second, indirect rule distributes responsibility. Decisions are attributed to offices and procedures, not to a single will. Subjects encounter judges, clerks, collectors, and councils more often than they encounter the ruler. Authority is insulated because it is less personalized. Conflict localizes. Anger disperses. Resentment attaches to process, not to the sovereign himself.

Indirect rule also stabilizes obedience. People comply more readily with systems than with commands.[140] Law feels different from decree. The office feels different from coercion. Procedure produces an appearance of neutrality even when outcomes are unequal or severe. Machiavelli notes that legitimacy often consolidates through regularity: when decisions follow recognizable forms, they appear less arbitrary. Even unfavorable outcomes are endured more readily when they seem impersonal. Habit is one of the strongest forces in political life.

Institutions convert force into procedure. Courts transform coercion into judgment.[141] Punishment becomes a sentence. What would otherwise require continuous enforcement is absorbed into the process. Coercive power remains present as a guarantee, but it no longer dominates daily experience.

In Christendom, this conversion of coercion into procedure had been accomplished over centuries primarily by ecclesiastical institutions — canon law, Church courts, parish discipline, and the confessional[142] — so that by Machiavelli's time the most elaborate infrastructure of indirect rule in Europe was not the apparatus of any secular state but the Church's own administrative machinery, which secular rulers had simultaneously borrowed, competed with, and depended upon.

THE EPISCOPAL APPARATUS IN PRACTICE

The diocesan system that governed Christian Europe was the most sophisticated intermediary structure on the continent. A bishop ruled a territory that might encompass hundreds of parishes across thousands of square miles.[143] He could not personally hear every case, visit every community, or discipline every errant priest.

---

[140] Machiavelli, *Discourses*, I.2; Weber, *Economy and Society*, 212–217.

[141] Berman, *Law and Revolution*, 120–164.

[142] Harold J. Berman, *Law and Revolution: The Formation of the Western Legal Tradition* (Cambridge, MA: Harvard University Press, 1983).

[143] Hamilton, *Religion in the Medieval West*; Brundage, *Medieval Canon Law.*

He governed, instead, through a layered chain of officials whose discretion was at once the system's operative mechanism and its permanent vulnerability.

The bishop's immediate administrative instrument was the chancellor — a trained canon lawyer who managed the diocesan court (the consistory), maintained the bishop's correspondence, kept the registers of ordinations and benefices, and in practice made most of the decisions that the bishop's name authorized.

Below the chancellor, archdeacons administered sub-diocesan territories, each holding visitational authority over the parishes within their jurisdiction. Below the archdeacons, rural deans coordinated clusters of parishes whose priests reported upward through them. A dispute originating in a village chapel over a disputed marriage or a priest's conduct traveled through this chain — rural dean to archdeacon to consistory court — and could be resolved, documented, and enforced without the bishop's personal involvement at any stage.

The diocesan court was the working face of this authority. It heard cases in canon law: marriage validity, testamentary disputes, clerical discipline, debt contracts made under oath, defamation cases where a party's Christian reputation was at stake. Its jurisdiction was not peripheral to daily life but central to it, because canon law governed exactly the domains — family, property, promise, reputation — that touched ordinary subjects most directly.

A man contesting his father's will, a woman seeking to establish the validity of a clandestine marriage, a merchant whose business partner had defaulted on a sworn agreement — all appeared before the consistory court, not before any secular tribunal. The bishop's indirect authority reached into these lives not through proclamation but through procedure.

The visitation system extended episcopal oversight further. Archdeacons were required to conduct periodic visitations of parishes within their territories — inspecting churches, questioning priests, receiving complaints from parishioners, and reporting findings upward. The visitation was both administrative and disciplinary: it assessed whether the church building was properly maintained, whether the priest was resident and conducting services, whether the sacraments were being administered correctly, and whether any moral disorders had developed in the parish community. The resulting records — visitation returns, detailing what was found and what corrective action was ordered — constituted the diocesan system's memory, accumulating across decades into a documentary record of pastoral conditions across the territory.

The confessional completed the structure by extending indirect rule into the interior life. Through the annual requirement of confession introduced by the Fourth Lateran Council in 1215,[144] every adult Christian became subject to an annual encounter with a priest who was empowered to assess conduct, impose penance, and withhold absolution.

The confessor was the system's deepest intermediary — the point at which ecclesiastical authority reached past external behavior into internal disposition. What the consistory court could not reach, the confessional could: not just actions but intentions, not just public violations but private ones, not just what subjects had done but what they had thought about doing.

The manuals written to guide confessors — the summae confessorum that trained priests across Europe in the late medieval period — were themselves instruments of standardization: they ensured that the discretion exercised at the confessional followed consistent principles instead of varying arbitrarily with each priest's judgment.

When secular rulers borrowed these structures, they were not copying an administrative model in the abstract. They were absorbing a specific and highly developed technology of indirect rule: trained officials holding defined jurisdictions, documentary record-keeping that gave authority institutional memory, a court system that converted enforcement into procedure, and a formation system that ensured the discretion exercised by intermediaries remained bounded.

The chanceries of secular princes were staffed by men trained in the same canon law schools that produced episcopal chancellors. The administrative records of medieval kingdoms followed the same documentary conventions that ecclesiastical record-keeping had developed. Secular courts adopted procedural norms — the right to be heard, rules of evidence, the requirement of reasoned judgment — that canonists had elaborated. What emerged was not two parallel

[144] Tentler, *Sin and Confession*; Tanner, *Decrees of the Ecumenical Councils*, Lateran IV, Canon 21 (245).

administrative systems but one shared administrative culture that expressed itself in both ecclesiastical and secular forms, with the Church having built the technology first.

Intermediaries also absorb friction. Ministers translate command into policy. Local officials adapt central directives to local conditions.[145] Each layer mediates conflict, normalizes authority, and reduces the need for constant intervention from the center. Coercion shifts from foreground instrument to background guarantee. Power grows quieter and more durable.

This layering contains conflict by channeling it. A judge can be appealed. A tax can be negotiated. A regulation can be delayed or revised. These processes redirect anger into forms that preserve the structure of rule. Instead of rebellion, there is a petition. Instead of revolt, litigation. Instead of conspiracy, maneuvering within offices. Machiavelli treats this as political containment: conflict persists, but it becomes governable.

Indirect rule also shields the ruler. Unpopular measures can be attributed to law, tradition, necessity, or institutional process. Even severe outcomes can appear compelled, not chosen. Subjects endure hardship more easily when it appears unavoidable. Machiavelli therefore treats legitimacy as shaped less by perceived justice alone than by perceived inevitability and coherence.

Indirect rule requires maintenance. Intermediaries develop interests of their own. Offices accumulate power.[146] Procedures harden into obstacles. Local officials drift. Distance protects authority, and it also obscures reality: information is filtered, failures are concealed, and responsibility dissolves into process. The ruler risks governing a diagram instead of conditions on the ground.

Sustaining indirect rule depends on an unstable balance. Intermediaries must be supervised without humiliation, empowered without autonomy, and disciplined without provoking collective resistance. Selection, rotation, and accountability become central tools. Officials must depend on the center for position and advancement while remaining credible to those they govern.

[145] Strayer, *Medieval Origins*, 35–60.

[146] Machiavelli, *Discourses*, I.34.

Indirect rule is the refinement of power through design. As administrative structures develop, raw coercion can recede from daily visibility even as its effectiveness increases. Power that must constantly announce itself signals fragility.

Machiavelli presents indirect rule as political evolution. Large, diverse, contentious societies endure through institutions that shape the channels through which decisions flow.[147] This is the quiet architecture of lasting authority: power survives by being embedded in offices, routines, and expectations — everywhere present even when it is nowhere theatrical.

[147] Strayer, *Medieval Origins*, 9–60.

CHAPTER 12

Reputation and Public Credibility

Political authority draws on more than coercion. It rests on what people believe about those who govern them: strength, competence, reliability, and legitimacy.[148] Machiavelli treats this domain under the heading of reputation and regards it as one of the most decisive forces in political life. Power operates through capacity, and through expectation — often before any command is issued or any punishment enforced.

Reputation functions as a form of political pre-commitment. Expectations shape behavior in advance of action. Subjects anticipate consequences, allies calculate reliability, and rivals estimate risk. These anticipations govern conduct long before authority is tested directly. Where reputation is strong, obedience often occurs without confrontation. Where it weakens, every decision becomes a test, and every exercise of authority carries disproportionate risk.

For Machiavelli, reputation is structural. It operates upstream of enforcement.[149] Long before laws are applied or armies mobilized, judgments form about how authority will respond to defiance, disorder, or crisis. These judgments organize political life in advance, determining whether resistance appears worthwhile, whether compliance seems prudent, and whether neutrality can be sustained. Most of the time, political systems run on belief.

Reputation therefore functions as power in its own right by shaping when coercion must be used at all. Authority that governs expectations can remain comparatively quiet; authority that fails to do so turns every moment into a contest. Heavy reliance on force is often a downstream signal: credibility has begun to fray, and enforcement must compensate for what belief no longer supplies.

Fear can compel obedience briefly, but fear without credibility produces instability. People comply temporarily while observing closely. They watch for hesitation, inconsistency, or excess. Once these appear, fear drains away. Authority

---

148 Machiavelli, *The Prince*, chs. 17–19; Skinner, *Foundations*, 130–168.
149 Machiavelli, *The Prince*, chs. 17, 19.

that depends on fear alone faces a ratchet: it must escalate continually, and escalation accelerates collapse.

Appearances matter as the medium through which legitimacy operates. Most people do not encounter power through abstract policy or constitutional theory. They encounter it through visible signs: ceremonies, public speech, symbolic acts, judicial outcomes, military posture, and the everyday conduct of officials.[150] These signals do more than communicate decisions. They teach interpretation. They instruct subjects how to read authority — what it values, what it tolerates, what it fears, and what it will defend.

Power is experienced narratively. Authority therefore manages meaning alongside outcomes. A ruler's reputation is shaped as much by consistency as by action. Predictable enforcement creates confidence. Unpredictable severity produces anxiety. Selective leniency reads as arbitrariness. Authority that shifts posture without an intelligible frame erodes belief even when outcomes are favorable. Credibility rests on coherence. Authority must make sense to those who live under it.

Scandal is dangerous because it fractures coherence. It exposes gaps between moral language and actual behavior.[151] When rulers speak of justice while acting unjustly, of discipline while indulging excess, or of piety while practicing corruption, authority becomes suspect. Obedience turns conditional. Loyalty becomes transactional. Compliance that once occurred automatically must now be purchased through concession or threat.

BONIFACE VIII AND THE ANATOMY OF REPUTATION COLLAPSE

The career of Pope Boniface VIII, who held the papacy from 1294 to 1303, offers the clearest documented case of reputation collapse in the medieval record[152] — and one that Machiavelli would have known through the historical accounts available to him. Boniface entered the papacy with the full institutional weight of the medieval Church behind him: an experienced canonist, a capable

[150] Clifford Geertz, *Local Knowledge* (New York: Basic Books, 1983).
[151] Kantorowicz, *King's Two Bodies*, 42–86.
[152] Boase, *Boniface VIII*, chaps. 8–12; Tierney, *Crisis of Church and State*, 172–192.

administrator, and the holder of the office that had successfully humiliated emperors at Canossa two centuries earlier. Within nine years that authority was in ruins. The mechanism was not military defeat or heresy. It was the systematic destruction of his public credibility by the French crown, executed through exactly the instruments this chapter has been describing.

The conflict began as a jurisdictional dispute. Philip IV of France had begun taxing the French clergy to fund a war, and Boniface issued the bull Clericis laicos in 1296 prohibiting clergy from paying taxes to secular rulers without papal consent. Philip responded by banning the export of gold and silver from France, cutting off a significant portion of the papacy's revenue. Boniface backed down. The capitulation was the first reputational damage: it demonstrated that the most powerful institutional claim in Christendom — papal supremacy over temporal rulers in matters of conscience — would yield under financial pressure. Rivals and subjects noted what he would actually defend and what he would not.

The second and more decisive phase began in 1301, when Philip arrested a French bishop on charges of treason and heresy and tried him in a royal court, directly challenging papal jurisdiction over clergy. Boniface responded with the bull Unam Sanctam in 1302, asserting in the strongest terms ever committed to a papal document that submission to the pope was necessary for salvation — that secular authority was subordinate to spiritual authority in all things, including the temporal governance of kingdoms. It was the maximum claim of the medieval papacy, issued at the moment when Boniface's capacity to enforce any claim was already in question. The distance between the assertion and the reality was itself reputationally catastrophic: the larger the claim, the more visible the gap between what authority declared and what it could actually compel.

Philip's minister Guillaume de Nogaret then executed what was, in effect, a reputation campaign. Pamphlets circulated accusations against Boniface that were carefully calibrated to damage him on the grounds of his own legitimacy claims: simony in acquiring the papal office, heresy in his private beliefs, sexual misconduct, sorcery. Whether any of these charges had factual basis was less important than their structural purpose, which was to establish that Boniface did not meet the moral standards through which he justified his own authority. The campaign was not aimed at defeating him in argument. It was aimed at making him appear ridiculous — at making the gap between his claims and his conduct so public and so vivid that the claims themselves became impossible to take seriously. In September 1303, Nogaret and an Italian ally physically seized Boniface at Anagni. He was released after three days but died the following month, his authority in tatters.

The aftermath is what concerns this chapter. The papacy that emerged from the Boniface catastrophe had lost something that legal vindication could not restore: the automatic deference that had once made its claims effective before enforcement was necessary. The next several decades saw the papacy relocate to Avignon under French influence, generating the perception — which was also a reputational verdict — that the office claiming universal spiritual authority was in practice a client of one European crown. That perception fed directly into the conditions that produced the Great Schism. Machiavelli, reading this history, would have recognized the pattern precisely: an authority that overreached its actual capacity, then failed to defend what it had claimed, then became the object of a systematic campaign to make its moral language look fraudulent. The credibility that had taken centuries to build had been spent in less than a decade, and the institution was still managing the consequences when he was born.

◆

In Christian Europe, where legitimacy was deeply moralized, these contradictions carried particular weight.[153] Authority was justified through virtue, faith, and divine order. Public violation of these claims was institutional damage, not merely personal failure. Scandal radiated outward, weakening confidence in the ruler and in the offices, laws, and traditions associated with that authority. A single visible breach could contaminate the structure.

The Western Schism had demonstrated this at maximum scale: once the papacy's conduct became sufficiently scandalous to multiple European kingdoms simultaneously, the credibility of the institution itself — not merely of its current occupant — collapsed, and no amount of legitimate-sounding decree could restore it until the constitutional crisis was resolved by other means.

This is the institutional realism behind Machiavelli's attention to moral language and public conduct. In a society whose legitimacy structures are

---

[153] Kantorowicz, *King's Two Bodies*, 193–232.

saturated with moral meaning, authority must remain morally intelligible in order to remain politically effective.

Reputation is not sustained by performance alone, and it is not sustained by rhetoric alone. It accumulates over time. Minor inconsistencies can be absorbed; persistent contradiction corrodes credibility. Over time, behavior outweighs proclamation. When action repeatedly contradicts the moral register used to justify rule, symbolic repair loses force.

Machiavelli therefore treats reputation as fragile political capital. It is built through visible competence, consistency under pressure, and restraint in success. Rash cruelty damages it. Excessive mercy damages it. Both extremes signal loss of control. Effective authority projects measured strength — capable of severity, but able to govern without constant severity. Reputation, once lost, is difficult to recover. Institutions can often be rebuilt faster than belief.

Public credibility also shapes external relations. Allies commit more readily to rulers perceived as reliable.[154] Rivals hesitate when authority appears resolute. Reputation operates beyond borders, influencing diplomacy, deterrence, and alliance formation. Foreign policy, in Machiavelli's account, is reputation magnified. A state known for inconsistency invites challenge. A state known for resolve discourages it.

Reputation, however, tracks reality over time. It cannot substitute indefinitely for strength, resources, or institutional capacity. Appearances unsupported by substance collapse under pressure. Reputation amplifies power; it does not generate it. A weak state cannot sustain a strong reputation for long. Strong states that neglect credibility squander their advantages.

Power that is credible can remain comparatively inactive. Power that lacks credibility must act constantly — and often fails even then. Political stability therefore depends on more than law and force. Law requires belief to function smoothly. Force requires legitimacy to remain effective. Without public credibility, institutions hollow out, procedures lose authority, and compliance becomes strategic rather than habitual.

---

[154] Machiavelli, *The Prince*, ch. 21.

Collapse rarely arrives dramatically. It arrives quietly, as belief erodes and obedience thins. To govern, in Machiavelli's sense, is to remain believable.

CHAPTER 13

Faction and Institutional Design

Machiavelli begins from a simple premise: political life is shaped by enduring conflict.[155] Wherever human beings pursue honor, wealth, influence, or security, rival interests form. These rivalries follow from the structure of desire and position, not from a temporary lapse in virtue or understanding. Faction, in Machiavelli's account, belongs to politics as a permanent condition.

This premise governs how political systems should be built, judged, and repaired. Analysis starts from friction. Human beings differ in capacity, ambition, vulnerability, and rank, and those differences generate competing claims over resources, status, protection, and authority. Formal equality can coexist with unequal outcomes; shared ideals can coexist with divergent interests. Conflict arises from within social life as it actually operates.[156]

This stance puts Machiavelli alongside—and against—older pictures of political health. Classical philosophy often described the just city as one in which reason aligns private appetite with the common good. Christian moral discourse frequently interprets discord through sin and pride and imagines its remedy in discipline or renewal.[157] Machiavelli treats moral aspiration as real and valuable while refusing to make it the load-bearing foundation of order. A political system that depends on sustained virtue for ordinary functioning becomes fragile under pressure.[158]

Harmony, in his analysis, offers limited diagnostic value.[159] Apparent unity can reflect exhaustion, fear, or silence — not durable agreement. Grievances often persist beneath the surface until a trigger forces them into view, and then rupture can be sudden and violent. Programs aimed at producing unanimity frequently redirect conflict into darker channels without converting it into stability.

---

155 Machiavelli, *Discourses on Livy*, I.4–6.

156 Machiavelli, *Discourses on Livy*, I.4–5; J. G. A. Pocock, *The Machiavellian Moment* (Princeton: Princeton University Press, 1975).

157 Thomas Aquinas, *De Regno*, I.1–2; Aristotle, *Politics*, III.6–7.

158 Machiavelli, *Discourses on Livy*, III.18.

159 Machiavelli, *Discourses on Livy*, I.4.

When conflict loses lawful outlets, it intensifies. Rivalries become more personal, more opaque, and more difficult to constrain. Political struggle continues, but it migrates into informal networks, conspiracies, and coercive bargains. Regimes that prize unanimity often prove brittle because their stability rests on pressure, not balance; when containment fails, release is catastrophic.

From here Machiavelli's central institutional insight follows: political order organizes struggle. Authority endures when conflict is anticipated, structured, and constrained within forms that keep it from becoming destructive.[160] Disorder emerges when disagreement lacks recognized paths of expression. When institutions cannot process conflict, conflict begins to process institutions.

Political systems therefore deserve judgment less by their surface calm than by their capacity to handle opposition. Visible contestation can signal functional containment. Machiavelli's admiration for the Roman Republic reflects this logic — and that he reached for Rome instead of Christendom's own institutional record was itself a diagnostic judgment: the very moralization of political conflict in Christian Europe had made it systematically harder for Christian polities to acknowledge conflict as a permanent condition requiring institutional management, not spiritual remedy.[161] Rome grew powerful by building mechanisms that brought social tension into durable channels.

The rivalry between patricians and plebeians became a force managed through tribunes, assemblies, vetoes, and appeals.[162] These institutions compelled negotiation, slowed domination, and prevented advantage from hardening into permanence. Rome's laws emerged from pressure and contestation, and political development proceeded through response and adjustment, never through ideal design.

The lesson is institutional, not moralistic: durable systems absorb political passions and convert them into structured competition.[163] When ambition lacks lawful outlets, it turns conspiratorial. When the opposition lacks a voice, it turns revolutionary. When power concentrates without counterweight, it turns predatory. These dynamics follow most reliably from control without channeling.

---

[160] Machiavelli, *Discourses on Livy*, I.4–5.
[161] Machiavelli, *Discourses on Livy*, I.4–6.
[162] Machiavelli, *Discourses on Livy*, I.4–6.
[163] Machiavelli, *Discourses on Livy*, I.4–5.

Institutional design becomes a problem of containment and conversion. Rivalry can be converted into competition, resentment into participation, ambition into office.[164] Elections, councils, courts, and appeals function as instruments of delay, diffusion, and mediation. They fragment conflict, redirect it, and make it survivable.

Effective institutions perform several functions at once. They make conflict visible without making it decisive, and they permit opposition without allowing domination. They also make loss tolerable.[165] A faction that loses an election retains the prospect of future victory; a class that loses a legal dispute retains standing inside the system. Defeat produces frustration, not annihilation. Stability depends less on permanent winners than on bearable loss.

Institutional mechanisms also degrade over time. Structures built to contain factions can begin to serve it. Offices accumulate privilege; temporary powers settle into permanence; procedures designed for balance become tools of capture; legal complexity becomes exclusion where it once provided mediation. Decay is incremental.[166] Each exception appears reasonable. Over time, institutions shift from channeling conflict to entrenching it.

During this shift, faction hardens into structure and power migrates from open contestation to quiet monopolization. Periodic correction becomes the price of endurance.

Political systems therefore need pathways for renewal before pressure becomes explosive. Renewal can take many forms—legal reform, institutional redesign, redistribution of authority, reassertion of founding arrangements. The governing question is whether balance can be restored, not how.

Where peaceful correction remains possible, crises can be reduced in frequency and intensity. Where correction becomes impossible, adjustment arrives through rupture.[167] Institutions then appear less as sacred inheritances than as functional instruments whose legitimacy rests on performance over time.

---

[164] Machiavelli, *Discourses on Livy*, III.6.

[165] Machiavelli, *Discourses on Livy*, I.4–5.

[166] Machiavelli, *Discourses on Livy*, III.1, III.18.

[167] Machiavelli, *Discourses on Livy*, III.1.

Large political communities tend instead toward equilibrium: a dynamic balance among forces that remain in tension. Stability is managed movement, sustained through maintenance, adjustment, and redesign. Endurance depends less on virtue, consensus, or goodwill than on the realism of institutional architecture. Political failure follows most often when systems are designed for people as they ought to be and not for people as they are.[168]

[168] Niccolò Machiavelli, *The Prince*, trans. Harvey C. Mansfield (Chicago: University of Chicago Press, 1998), ch. 15; Machiavelli, *Discourses on Livy*, I.3.

PART IV

COERCION AND LEGITIMACY

If Part III explains how rule operates, Part IV clarifies what allows it to endure. No political system survives on coercion alone, and no political system survives on moral language alone. Christendom's distinctive condition is that legitimacy is moralized while enforcement remains unavoidable. Authority must therefore operate within a persistent tension: rulers are required to appear righteous in order to command obedience, yet they must also govern through constraints that righteousness by itself cannot supply.

Machiavelli is often invoked as a theorist of force. He is more accurately read as an analyst of its limits. He observes that violence can seize a city and still fail to govern it; it can punish dissent and still generate hatred; it can impose order briefly and still erode the legitimacy that makes order durable. The central question is therefore how force interacts with credibility, conscience, testimony, and long-term allegiance.

Part IV examines this interaction directly. It distinguishes coercion that stabilizes from coercion that corrodes. It also examines forms of power that operate without constant enforcement — formation, persuasion, habituation, and moral interiority — as governance mechanisms that extend authority beyond the reach of continual command.

In Christendom, this interaction is especially complex because obedience is rarely singular. Subjects are shaped by multiple, overlapping loyalties: religious obligation, civic identity, dynastic allegiance, local faction, family honor, and communal memory. These claims compete for priority in the conscience. Political authority must negotiate with existing structures of belief and duty that it neither fully controls nor can easily suppress.

The two chapters that follow divide this territory precisely. Chapter 14 examines coercion directly: how force functions as a substitute for authority, the predictable trajectory through which reliance on enforcement accelerates the erosion it attempts to prevent, and where Machiavelli locates the alternative — in formation, the slow process through which authority becomes internalized instead of merely obeyed. Chapter 15 examines the specific complexity of rival loyalties in Christendom: how authority must negotiate the layered obligations — religious, civic, familial, professional — that subjects carry before they encounter any political command, and how durable political order organizes that plurality without suppressing it. Coercion appears in both chapters as one instrument among others — necessary, dangerous, and always limited.

The purpose of this analysis is neither to excuse coercion nor to romanticize conscience. It is to show why legitimacy functions as an operational resource; why moral language serves as political infrastructure; and why stable systems depend on managing both force and belief, sanction and meaning, command and consent.

Power endures, in Machiavelli's account, not when it is most feared and not when it is most admired, but when it becomes expected. Part IV examines how that expectation is produced, sustained, and lost.

CHAPTER 14

THE LIMITS OF FORCE

Power is often confused with the capacity to compel obedience. In moments of crisis this confusion intensifies.[169] When institutions falter and social order appears fragile, leaders reach for force: stricter laws, harsher penalties, expanded surveillance, tighter controls. Force promises speed. It appears decisive. Under pressure, it feels like control.

Force, however, functions as a substitute for authority, and it carries a high cost.[170]

Coercion suppresses behavior without generating legitimacy. It produces compliance without loyalty.[171] Authority draws on shared belief, internalized norms, and institutional habit; coercion relies on threat. As threats weaken through exhaustion, resistance, resource limits, or declining credibility, obedience thins. Political order endures because most people comply most of the time even when enforcement is absent.

No institution commands sufficient coercive capacity to regulate every action of every member.[172] Surveillance expands unevenly. Punishment intensifies selectively. Control remains partial. When compliance depends primarily on enforcement, breakdown unfolds gradually.[173] Rules require constant policing. Norms lose binding force. Authority becomes visible everywhere because it no longer operates quietly anywhere.

Coercion applies pressure from the outside. Authority shapes behavior continuously. As reliance on enforcement increases, the absence of authority becomes more apparent. Commands grow louder as consent thins out. Penalties

---

[169] Hannah Arendt, *On Violence* (New York: Harcourt, Brace & World, 1970), 35–56.

[170] Niccolò Machiavelli, *The Prince*, trans. Harvey C. Mansfield (Chicago: University of Chicago Press, 1998), chs. 8, 17–19.

[171] Machiavelli, *The Prince*, chs. 17, 19; Niccolò Machiavelli, *Discourses on Livy*, trans. Harvey C. Mansfield (Chicago: University of Chicago Press, 1996), III.6.

[172] Weber, "*Politics as a Vocation*," 78–94.

[173] Machiavelli, *The Prince*, ch. 19; Weber, "*Politics as a Vocation*," 78–83.

multiply as legitimacy erodes. Systems governed primarily through threat reach their peak of visibility as their foundations weaken.

Surface obedience masks deeper effects. Fear, resentment, and calculation replace internal commitment.[174] Individuals learn how to navigate the system instead of sustaining it. Compliance becomes selective. Evasion becomes strategic. Rules appear as obstacles, not guides. Over time, institutions organized around coercion hollow themselves out and persist by pressure alone.

Political collapse rarely arrives as a single event. Empires decline as enforcement grows more visible and legitimacy recedes. By the time coercion dominates public life, authority has already lost its stabilizing role. Machiavelli recognized the necessity of force under extraordinary conditions while treating it as a provisional instrument, never a governing foundation.

Coercion follows a predictable trajectory. It strains institutional capacity. Continuous enforcement consumes resources through expanding surveillance, proliferating penalties, and growing bureaucratic apparatus. Energy shifts from governing purpose to monitoring compliance. The institution begins to consume the society it once ordered.[175]

Coercion reshapes social relations. Obedience attaches to observation, not obligation. Responsibility gives way to calculation. Trust erodes. Solidarity weakens. Relationships reorganize around enforcement and evasion instead of shared commitment.

Coercion also accelerates instability. Each escalation yields diminishing returns.[176] Resistance increases as pressure rises. Institutions misread this response as defiance when it is actually decay, and intensify enforcement, deepening the cycle they seek to control.

Durable political orders rest on legitimacy.[177] Legitimacy takes the form of a shared belief that the system merits maintenance even when it imposes cost, constraint, and sacrifice. This belief develops through cultivation, not command.

---

[174] Machiavelli, *The Prince*, chs. 17, 19.

[175] Michael Mann, *The Sources of Social Power*, vol. 1 (Cambridge: Cambridge University Press, 1986), 1–33.

[176] Machiavelli, *The Prince*, ch. 19; Weber, "*Politics as a Vocation*," 78–83.

[177] Niccolò Machiavelli, *Discourses on Livy*, trans. Harvey C. Mansfield (Chicago: University of Chicago Press, 1996), I.4–5; Weber, "*Politics as a Vocation*," 78–83.

As legitimacy weakens, institutions choose between reform and repression. Repression extends time horizons without producing stability. It freezes conflict without resolving it.[178] Displays of strength—surveillance, punishment, spectacle—mask structural fragility without repairing it.

Machiavelli locates durability elsewhere: in formation.

Authority endures when individuals are shaped—gradually, collectively, and persistently—into roles, expectations, and obligations aligned with institutional order. Formation works through family, education, religion, law, professional norms, narrative, and ritual.[179] It produces disposition, not mere compliance. It creates people who govern themselves.

Where formation is strong, enforcement remains limited. Where formation weakens, enforcement expands. Enduring orders devote far more energy to shaping behavior than to punishing deviation. The visible instruments of force remain secondary to the invisible processes of socialization.

This orientation explains Machiavelli's attention to religion, reputation, custom, law, and institutional habit. Authority stabilizes long before force is required. Coercion functions as a reserve instrument. Formation establishes the conditions of rule.

As legitimacy erodes, leaders gravitate toward control. Rules tighten. Penalties multiply. Enforcement expands. Each measure signals command while accelerating decay.

Power endures when it becomes expected—embedded in habit, reinforced by norm, and sustained through shared understanding.[180]

Coercion can seize a moment. Formation sustains an age.

---

[178] Machiavelli, *Discourses on Livy*, I.18; III.1.

[179] Machiavelli, *Discourses on Livy*, I.11–12; John Bossy, *Christianity in the West 1400–1700* (Oxford: Oxford University Press, 1985), 1–25.

[180] Machiavelli, *The Prince*, ch. 17; Niccolò Machiavelli, *Discourses on Livy*, I.3.

CHAPTER 15

MANAGING RIVAL LOYALTIES

Political orders operate across multiple forms of allegiance. Individuals belong simultaneously to families, faiths, cities, professions, classes, and political communities.[181] Each affiliation carries obligations, expectations, emotional attachments, and moral claims. Political stability emerges from how these loyalties are organized and ranked, not from their elimination.

This condition is a durable feature of political life. Long before the emergence of nation-states, human beings navigated overlapping obligations that competed for priority.[182] What varies across history is the institutional capacity to manage this plurality without collapse. Where such capacity is weak, authority fragments. Where it is strong, plurality becomes governable.

Machiavelli's world was shaped by this complexity. A Florentine citizen might owe loyalty to a ruling family, obedience to republican law, devotion to the Church, fidelity to kin, and honor to a guild at the same time. These commitments functioned as lived obligations enforced through reputation, sanction, material dependence, moral judgment, and, at times, violence. Governance operated within their friction, never above them.

Rival loyalties generate political danger when they issue incompatible demands without a recognized hierarchy.[183] A ruler may command an action that collides with religious conscience. Civic duty may press against family interest. Professional obligation may undermine state policy. Without a shared framework for ranking these claims, authority loses coherence. Obedience becomes selective as individuals comply where loyalties align and resist where they collide.

Fragmentation rarely appears all at once. It begins with hesitation, delay, procedural ambiguity, and uneven enforcement. Over time, these ambiguities

---

[181] Susan Reynolds, *Kingdoms and Communities in Western Europe 900–1300* (Oxford: Oxford University Press, 1984), 1–40.
[182] Michael Walzer, *Spheres of Justice* (New York: Basic Books, 1983), 3–30.
[183] Ernst H. Kantorowicz, *The King's Two Bodies* (Princeton: Princeton University Press, 1957), 193–232; Niccolò Machiavelli, *Discourses on Livy*, trans. Harvey C. Mansfield and Nathan Tarcov (Chicago: University of Chicago Press, 1996), I.4–5.

harden into factional alignment. Institutions shift from neutral arbitration toward group interest.[184] Law loses coherence as interpretation follows allegiance. Courts diverge. Commands circulate with uneven effect. Authority loses its unified voice as the underlying order fractures.

Machiavelli treats this process as resistant to moral exhortation. Appeals to unity falter when they contradict lived obligation. Family, faith, and honor retain their force regardless of political abstraction. Efforts to impose exclusive loyalty through force intensify resistance, transforming ordinary pluralism into existential conflict. Complex societies sustain allegiance through arrangement, not absolutism.

Effective governance organizes rival loyalties instead of attempting their removal. Institutions perform this work through hierarchy, jurisdiction, and procedure. Law assigns authority to defined domains.[185] Religious institutions articulate the boundaries of conscience. Civic offices delimit public obligation. Economic structures regulate professional loyalty. Courts adjudicate conflicts by assigning priority without denying plurality.

When these arrangements function well, conflicts of allegiance remain bounded. Individuals fulfill multiple obligations without permanent contradiction. Loyalty becomes layered, not exclusive. Authority gains credibility by acknowledging the complexity of belonging and providing workable pathways through it. Political order is preserved through structure, not simplification[186].

This ordering requires continual maintenance. It is taught, reinforced, and periodically revised. Education socializes individuals into a grammar of obligation by clarifying what is owed, when, and to whom.[187] Long before adulthood, individuals learn to distinguish family claims from civic ones, conscience from command, and private loyalty from public law.

---

[184] Niccolò Machiavelli, *Discourses on Livy*, I.7, I.18; Quentin Skinner, *The Foundations of Modern Political Thought*, vol. 1 (Cambridge: Cambridge University Press, 1978), 130–138.
[185] Brian Tierney, *The Crisis of Church and State 1050–1300* (Toronto: University of Toronto Press, 1988), 1–30.
[186] Susan Reynolds, *Kingdoms and Communities in Western Europe 900–1300*, 2nd ed. (Oxford: Clarendon Press, 1997), 40–80.
[187] Marcia L. Colish, *Medieval Foundations of the Western Intellectual Tradition* (New Haven: Yale University Press, 1997), 120–150.

Ritual and custom reinforce these distinctions through repetition, not argument. Oaths, ceremonies, offices, and public roles train perception. They habituate individuals to shifting registers of obligation depending on context. Loyalty becomes practiced, not merely felt. Political order reproduces itself through routine as much as through law.

Symbols play a central role because they operate at the level of meaning, not command. Flags, public holidays, shared histories, civic myths, religious ceremonies, and collective memory coordinate identity. They indicate which loyalty takes precedence when obligations collide and provide interpretive shortcuts when law alone proves insufficient.

In moments of crisis, symbolic hierarchy often carries greater weight than procedural clarity.[188] As institutions strain and routines falter, people turn to narratives that define belonging and obligation. Orders with confused or hollow symbols struggle to command allegiance under pressure. Competing symbols—rival oaths, moral languages, and claims of ultimacy—fracture allegiance at its deepest level. Political conflict shifts from policy to belonging.

Failures in managing rival loyalties produce predictable outcomes. Authority fractures along identity lines.[189] Jurisdiction blurs. Law becomes selective. Enforcement turns partisan. Violence expands from exception to justification. Civil conflict, secession, and chronic instability follow as structural consequences of unmanaged allegiance. When no authority can credibly rank obligations, every loyalty claims absolute priority.

Machiavelli's attention to this problem reflects his refusal to treat political subjects as abstract individuals. He understood people as layered beings who inherit identity before consenting to law and belong before obeying. Authority that ignores this layering mistakes formal command for effective power.

To govern is therefore to organize belonging. Successful systems integrate prior loyalties into a larger framework that limits their destructive potential. Family

---

[188] Machiavelli, *Discourses on Livy*, I.11–12; Clifford Geertz, "Centers, Kings, and Charisma," in *Local Knowledge* (New York: Basic Books, 1983), 121–146.
[189] Machiavelli, *Discourses on Livy*, I.7; III.6; Brucker, *The Civic World of Early Renaissance Florence*, 120–150.

loyalty remains respected and bound by law. Religious devotion is honored within civic order. Professional identity is encouraged and regulated by public obligation.

This integration depends on restraint. Authority that attempts to dominate every sphere provokes resistance from identities it cannot absorb. Authority that withdraws entirely leaves rival loyalties to compete violently. Stability emerges from calibrated intervention—knowing where to assert priority and where to defer.[190]

Tension persists. Conflict remains. What changes is its form. Rival loyalties become compatible enough to coexist without tearing the political order apart.

Loyalty, in this sense, functions as a political technology. It can be cultivated, structured, mismanaged, or weaponized. Institutions that understand this treat allegiance as material to be shaped, not sentiment to be assumed.

Where institutions succeed, individuals belong to multiple worlds without being forced into total choice. Where they fail, loyalty becomes a weapon and identity hardens into a fault line.

This chapter completes the book's examination of power within Christendom. Having traced force, legitimacy, institutions, formation, reputation, and allegiance, the inquiry now turns to a deeper substrate of political order: the narratives through which civilizations interpret authority, obligation, and human nature. Biblical narrative enters the analysis as a shared grammar through which legitimacy is imagined and contested.

---

[190] Machiavelli, *The Prince*, chs. 17, 19.

PART V

Scripture as Political Formation: A Case Study

Part V is a deliberate gear-shift. The preceding parts have moved through biography, institutional architecture, governance mechanics, and the specific dynamics of coercion and legitimacy — analytical territory most readers of this book will find immediately recognizable. Part V turns to Judges, Kingship, the Maccabean revolt, and Paul. For some readers this will feel like familiar ground entered from an unfamiliar direction. That disorientation is the point.

The exercise Part V proposes is defamiliarization. These texts are almost certainly known to you — through formation, liturgy, preaching, or scholarship. You know what they say theologically. The question Part V poses is different: what do they reveal when read as a political scientist would read them? Not as sacred narrative, not as spiritual formation, not as doctrinal source — but as case studies in the governance problems that recur in every political civilization. What happens to authority when there is no durable enforcement structure? How does a community purchase political consolidation and at what cost? What does legitimacy look like when the occupying power controls the institutional machinery? How is obedience reconstructed when the old coercive mechanisms are unavailable? These are Machiavelli's questions. They are also, it turns out, the questions these texts are already asking.

Before turning to the book's own broader application of this method, Part V must account for the instances where Machiavelli himself did the reading. Moses and David are the primary scriptural figures he analyzed directly—returning to the Exodus narrative and the Davidic consolidation to draw arguments about founding, force, and institutional survival that he regarded as among his clearest illustrations of political principle. Chapter 16 therefore occupies a foundational methodological position. It does not apply his framework to material he never addressed. It follows his analysis of Moses, reports what he found, and extends it into the civilizational context this book has been building throughout. While the book will apply his method to texts he largely left untouched—such as Judges, the Maccabean revolt, and the Pauline letters—it will return directly to his own biblical commentary when examining David.

The historical grounding for this reading is straightforward. In medieval and early modern Europe, Scripture was not primarily a private text. It was public infrastructure — heard in liturgy, memorized through the Psalter, cited in legal proceedings, invoked in political argument, and absorbed before most subjects ever encountered a political treatise. The biblical narratives examined here were not curiosities known to specialists. They were the shared grammar through which authority, obedience, revolt, and failure were understood by the civilization Machiavelli was analyzing. That grammar was operating inside him as much as it was operating around him.

The five chapters apply the framework across a sequence that moves between Machiavelli's own readings and the book's extensions of it. Chapter 16 examines what Machiavelli found in the Exodus narrative — founding violence, the armed prophet, the structural logic of cruelty used well — and establishes the analytical posture that the remaining chapters carry forward. Chapter 17 turns to Judges: governance without durable enforcement, and cyclical breakdown as the structural outcome of moral aspiration without institutional continuity. Chapter 18 examines Kingship: political consolidation and its costs, drawing directly on Machiavelli's unsentimental reading of King David to explore the permanent trade-off between justice and survival. Chapter 19 examines the Maccabean revolt: legitimacy under occupation, the collision between sacred law and foreign power, and the question of when resistance becomes obligation. Chapter 20 turns to Paul: authority reconstructed without coercion, formation and conscience as governance technologies, and the internalization of obedience as the mechanism that will later become Christendom's most durable institutional inheritance.

Each case isolates a governance problem and shows it working itself out in narrative. What the defamiliarization produces is doubled literacy. The reader who completes Part V has read these texts in two registers simultaneously — the theological register they already carried, and the political register the analytical framework supplies. That doubling is the formation payoff. It is also the precise condition in which Machiavelli read Moses. He did not choose between the sacred and the political. He inhabited both, because the civilization that formed him did not separate them. Part V trains the same double reading — and in doing so, it brings the reader closer to understanding what kind of mind produced *The Prince* and why.

CHAPTER 16

THE FOUNDING VIOLENCE OF MOSES

There is a passage in the second book of the Pentateuch that most readers have learned to read as a story about idolatry. Moses descends from Sinai carrying the tablets of the Law. The Israelites, in his absence, have made a calf of gold and are worshipping it. Moses reaches the foot of the mountain, sees what the people have done, and shatters the tablets on the ground. Then he does something that devotional reading tends to pass over quickly. He stands at the camp gate and calls out: *Who is on the Lord's side? Come to me.* The tribe of Levi steps forward. Moses tells them: *Each of you take your sword, move from gate to gate throughout the camp, and kill your brother, your companion, and your neighbor.* By the time the killing stops, approximately three thousand people are dead. The Levites are then consecrated as priests[191] — set apart for sacred service — as a direct consequence of what they have just done.

Machiavelli read this passage. He returned to it across multiple texts, and the argument he drew from it is one of the most clarifying things he ever wrote. What he found in Exodus 32 he found nowhere else in Scripture with the same precision[192] — a case study in the institutional logic of founding that confirmed, in a narrative the entire civilization around him was reading devotionally, everything he had argued about the relationship between law and the force that stands behind it.

The argument appears first in *The Prince*, Chapter VI, where Machiavelli assembles a short list of the greatest founders in human memory: Moses, Cyrus, Theseus, Romulus.[193] The company is deliberately mixed. A Hebrew lawgiver stands alongside a Persian conqueror, a Greek hero, and the founder of Rome. What they share is not religion, dynasty, or civilization. What they share is the

[191] Exodus 32:1–6, 26–29.
[192] de Grazia, *Machiavelli in Hell*, 54, 275; Strauss, *Thoughts on Machiavelli*, 51, 83–84, 114, 204–205.
[193] Machiavelli, *The Prince*, chap. 6.

structure of their problem. Each introduced a new order — new laws, new institutions, new obligations — into a world organized differently before. Each faced the same obstacle: those who benefited from the old arrangement would oppose the new one, and those who stood to gain from the new order would not defend it with conviction until they had seen it succeed.

Machiavelli's observation about this problem is among his most precise: the nature of peoples is variable — easy to persuade, hard to keep persuaded.[194] A founder can make his case. He can build initial consent. But belief erodes. Opponents regroup. The persuaded majority, whose commitment was always conditional, begins to waver the moment the new order encounters its first serious test. At that moment, the question is institutional, not rhetorical. What happens when people who once agreed stop complying?

Here is where Machiavelli divides the world. He distinguishes between prophets who are armed and prophets who are not.[195] Savonarola preached in Florence with extraordinary effect. He moved the population. He reshaped the city's public culture through the force of his moral conviction and the authority of his speech. Then Florence stopped believing in him, and he was destroyed.[196] He had no mechanism for sustaining the order he had built when persuasion ran out. His problem was not intelligence or sincerity but structure: he had nothing behind his words except more words.

Moses had something else. The tribe of Levi was standing at the gate.

◆

The deeper argument appears in the *Discourses on Livy*, where Machiavelli examines the Moses passage through the lens of institutional founding and its enemies.[197] Anyone who wishes to introduce a new order faces opposition not from the merely indifferent or the temporarily unconvinced, but from a specific and structurally predictable source: the envious — those whose position, influence, or advantage derived from the old arrangement, and who have concrete

194 Machiavelli, *The Prince*, chap. 6.
195 Machiavelli, *The Prince*, chap. 6.
196 Machiavelli, *The Prince*, chap. 6; Skinner, *Machiavelli*, 7–14.
197 Machiavelli, *Discourses*, III.30.

reasons to resist its replacement. Their opposition is rational, persistent, and not amenable to persuasion, because what they stand to lose is real.

Machiavelli uses the phrase *infiniti uomini* — countless men — to describe those Moses was compelled to kill.[198] The phrase is not casual hyperbole. It names the structural problem of founding precisely: the obstacle is not a single rival or a manageable faction. It is the class of constituted opponents embedded in the old order, whose interests are incompatible with the new one and who will continue to undermine it for as long as they remain. Against this kind of opposition, argument accomplishes nothing. The problem is not epistemic. It is structural. Removing it requires a structural solution.

Three thousand dead at the camp gate is Machiavelli's evidence that Moses understood this.

◆

The distinction Machiavelli draws elsewhere between cruelty used well and cruelty used badly is directly relevant here, and the Exodus episode is one of his clearest illustrations of the former. Cruelty used well — the phrase appears in *The Prince* in the analysis of Agathocles — is cruelty that is concentrated at the moment of founding, executed decisively, and then concluded.[199] It does not drag on. It does not become the governing logic of the new order. It is performed once, at the point of maximum institutional vulnerability, to remove the specific obstacle that cannot be removed any other way.

Cruelty used badly is the mirror image. It is scattered, ongoing, and unpredictable. It expands rather than contracts over time. It serves no founding purpose because it has no defined endpoint. It does not solve the structural problem. It sustains it indefinitely while adding fear to the conditions under which it must be managed.

Moses's action at the Golden Calf fits neither the normal ethical categories of the devotional tradition — divine judgment, proportionate response to apostasy — nor the merely strategic logic of a ruler clearing rivals from the board. It fits Machiavelli's third category: the founding violence of a lawgiver who has correctly

[198] Machiavelli, *Discourses*, III.30; Strauss, *Thoughts on Machiavelli*, 114.
[199] Machiavelli, *The Prince*, chap. 8.

identified the structural obstacle to his new order and has the capacity and will to remove it at the decisive moment. The Levites kill at the gate and then sheathe their swords. The episode closes. The Law is reinscribed on new tablets. The new order proceeds.

From a devotional perspective, the passage narrates divine judgment and priestly election. From Machiavelli's perspective, it narrates the institutional logic of every durable founding — the moment when the coercive capacity behind the new order is demonstrated clearly enough that future opposition becomes calculably suicidal.

There is a detail in the Exodus passage that Machiavelli's framework makes newly visible even where he does not linger on it explicitly: the killers are the Levites, and the Levites are the priestly tribe. Moses does not deploy an outside force. He asks, at the moment of crisis, *Who is on the Lord's side?* — and the answer is a tribal identity that is simultaneously a sacred lineage. The men who step forward at the gate are the men who will subsequently administer the sacrificial cult, the tabernacle, and the religious law. Sacred authority and coercive capacity are not two separate things in this episode. They are fused in the same institutional body.

The Levites earn their consecration by demonstrating their willingness to enforce the founding order. Their priestly authority is, in part, a recognition of their function as its armed guarantor.

This structural fusion is not incidental to the present book's argument. It is, as Chapter 2 established, the characteristic feature of Christendom as a political civilization — the feature that made it durable and volatile in equal measure. For a thousand years after the episode examined here, Christian institutions organized authority on the same underlying principle: the body that administers spiritual sanction is the body whose institutional weight makes political compliance possible.[200] Bishops exercise judicial authority. Church courts determine the legal status of marriage, inheritance, and obligation.[201] Excommunication is not merely a spiritual penalty — it dissolves the social bonds through which political and

[200] Berman, *Law and Revolution*, 85–119; Kantorowicz, *King's Two Bodies*, 42–52.
[201] Brundage, *Medieval Canon Law*, 56–100.

commercial life operate.[202] The Levites at the camp gate are not an archaic curiosity. They are an early instance of the governing structure Machiavelli spent his career watching operate, strain, and, in 1527, fail catastrophically.

What distinguishes Machiavelli's treatment of Moses from a theological reading is not the conclusions he reaches but the question he brings. He does not ask what the episode reveals about the nature of God, or what it demands of the faithful, or how it fits into the providential arc of Israel's history. He asks what it reveals about the institutional logic of founding a durable new order. That question — aimed at a text the entire civilization around him was reading through devotional categories — produces an answer the devotional framework could not generate.

This is not an act of hostility toward scripture; it is the same analytic attention Machiavelli brings to Livy. When he reads the Roman historians, he strips away the legendary overlay to ask what the political mechanics actually were — what institutional arrangements produced the outcomes, the narrative records, and what can be learned from them by anyone who has to build or sustain an institution under pressure. He reads Moses identically.

What made the Mosaic founding endure? Not the content of the Law. Not the sincerity of Moses's devotion, which Machiavelli does not dispute. What made it endure was the quality of the institutions Moses built and the willingness to use force at the moment when those institutions were most vulnerable.

This is what it means, in practice, to apply the effectual truth to scriptural narrative. The effectual truth is not what institutions announce themselves to be, or what moral authority underwrites them, or what the faithful believe about their origins. It is what they actually produce when tested[203] — whether enforcement holds, whether compliance is sustained beyond the moment of persuasion, whether the founding act generates durable order or merely deferred collapse. Tested against that standard, the episode at the camp gate is not primarily a story about sin and judgment — it is a story about the relationship between law and the force that stands behind it.

---

[202] Tierney, *Crisis of Church and State*, 1–40.
[203] Machiavelli, *The Prince*, chap. 15.

Two major lines of interpretation have organized scholarly discussion of Machiavelli's Moses passages. Harvey Mansfield's reading emphasizes the near-totality of the violence. Moses's command — kill your brother, your companion, your neighbor — crosses every prior social bond deliberately.[204] The point is that the new order's demands exceed the claims of existing loyalty. The killing is constitutive of the new community's moral universe, not merely instrumental to its founding.

Maurizio Viroli's reading is more narrowly institutional. Moses uses cruelty well in the technical Machiavellian sense: concentrated, purposeful, and concluded.[205] The violence solves a specific structural problem and is then closed. The consecration of the Levites that follows is the positive complement — enforcement capacity formally institutionalized rather than merely exercised.

Both readings illuminate something real, and the disagreement between them is less about Machiavelli's text than about what founding violence does to the ongoing life of institutions. For the argument of this book, the dispute can be held in suspension.

What matters is not whether Moses's killing was constitutive or instrumental. What matters is what Machiavelli's method makes possible: reading the foundational text of the Western religious tradition as political evidence. The question he brings to Exodus 32 is diagnostic, not devotional. And it produces something that centuries of theological commentary, precisely because of its categories, had systematically obscured.

Moses built the Law in stone. He built the enforcement behind it in flesh. The Levites consecrated for killing and the tablets inscribed with commandments are not two separate things. They are the two faces of a single institutional act — the founding of an order durable enough to survive the wavering of the people it was built to govern. The chapters that follow apply this same diagnostic question to

[204] Mansfield, *Machiavelli's Virtue*, 281–294.

[205] Viroli, *Machiavelli*, 91–99.

scriptural material Machiavelli never addressed. The question, once asked of Moses, does not stay contained.

CHAPTER 17

Judges and Political Instability

The Book of Judges is set in the period after Israel's entry into the land and before the establishment of monarchy. It unfolds as a sequence of crisis episodes rather than as a continuous national history.[206] There is no stable capital, no permanent executive, and no enduring administrative center. The figures called 'judges' function as ad hoc leaders — military deliverers, arbiters, and rallying figures — who arise in moments of danger and then recede, leaving little institutional residue behind.

Judges therefore preserve a sustained depiction of governance that never becomes ordinary. The book's famous refrain about everyone doing what seems right operates as a compressed political description. Authority remains local. Enforcement appears intermittently. Coordination proves fragile. The narrative returns to the same pattern — threat, mobilization, temporary relief, relapse — through repetition that serves diagnostic rather than ornamental purposes.[207] What the pattern illustrates is *necessità* as a governing condition rather than an exceptional one: when emergency leadership substitutes for durable structure, necessity does not recede after each crisis but becomes the permanent medium through which a community relates to its own survival.

This makes Judges a fitting starting point for Scripture read as political formation. It shows how a community can retain moral language, shared memory, and covenantal identity while drifting toward disorder when offices fail to persist, law lacks reliable enforcement, and no mechanism carries hard-won stability across generations. Instability appears as the predictable outcome of arrangements unable to sustain coherence over time.

Judges offers one of the most unsparing political portraits in the biblical canon. It records recurring failure: moral aspiration without enforcement, fragmented authority without coordination, and repeated crises without consolidation. Read

---

[206] Robert G. Boling, *Judges*, Anchor Bible 6A (Garden City, NY: Doubleday, 1975).
[207] Martin Noth, *The Deuteronomistic History* (Sheffield: JSOT Press, 1981).

as political anthropology instead of devotional narrative, Judges illuminates with unusual clarity the conditions under which societies drift toward disorder.

The book's refrain — 'In those days there was no king in Israel; everyone did what was right in his own eyes' — functions as a political diagnosis. It identifies the absence of centralized authority, enforceable law, and institutional continuity. The diagnosis operates by the standard Machiavelli would later name the *effectual truth*: what matters is not Israel's moral vocabulary or covenantal aspiration but what its political arrangements actually produce — which is a recognizable pattern of decentralized power struggling to sustain collective order.

That pattern defines the book's political logic. External pressure intensifies, internal cohesion weakens, and crisis produces a charismatic leader. Order is restored temporarily through force or improvisation.[208] When the leader disappears, authority dissipates and fragmentation returns. In Machiavelli's terms, what each judge possesses is *virtù* — the capacity to act decisively within a given configuration of forces — but *virtù* unsupported by institutional design cannot outlast the alignment of circumstances that made it effective. Each judge's authority is, in structural terms, a momentary coordination of capacity and *fortuna*: it holds as long as both align and collapse when either shifts. The system resets because nothing within it retains authority once the emergency passes.

Leadership in Judges is episodic and reactive. Authority arises through *necessità* instead of succession or office — which is Machiavelli's precise distinction between authority that is structurally grounded and authority that is circumstantially produced.[209] Loyalty attaches to circumstance, not structure. A judge commands obedience during a crisis but lacks institutional means to translate victory into lasting order. When the crisis ends — or when the judge dies — that authority evaporates. The central political problem exposed is the inability to institutionalize the good once recognized: to convert a temporary alignment of capacity and circumstance into a durable structure that persists without depending on the same alignment recurring.

---

208 Daniel I. Block, *Judges, Ruth, New American Commentary* (Nashville: Broadman & Holman, 1999).

209 Max Weber, *Economy and Society* (Berkeley: University of California Press, 1978).

The narrative affirms strong moral commitments — covenant, law, fidelity — while depicting a society in which those commitments lack durable enforcement.[210] Norms exist but are upheld unevenly. Law is known but applied inconsistently. Authority is acknowledged but exercised discontinuously. The people appear bound by obligation yet unable to stabilize it.

Moral vision remains present without political embodiment. Obedience becomes intermittent and conditional. Loyalty attaches to persons, not offices; to moments, not institutions. This is the condition Machiavelli treats as the signature vulnerability of systems that rely on individual *virtù* without institutional scaffolding: governance yields to improvisation, crisis management replaces rule, and leadership is evaluated by immediate effectiveness, never by the capacity to build continuity. Each generation confronts similar threats and relies on the same emergency solutions because no structure preserves gains across time.

Local power dominates this environment. Tribes, clans, and households function as semi-autonomous units, each guarding its own interests and loyalties.[211] Coordination across regions remains weak and episodic. Cooperation emerges primarily under existential threat. External enemies can be resisted collectively only under extreme pressure. Internal disputes escalate because no shared mechanism adjudicates them consistently. Victories achieved through force dissipate because no administrative or legal framework stabilizes outcomes.

Authority in Judges remains intensely personal. It adheres to individuals, not offices — which is, in Machiavelli's analysis, the foundational design failure.[212] Authority that cannot outlast its current occupant because it was never embedded in a role, a procedure, or an expectation draws loyalty through charisma, strength, or perceived divine favor: this grants it intensity in the moment and fragility over time. When the individual disappears, nothing carries authority forward. What Machiavelli would recognize as the office — the continuity mechanism that allows a political community to persist through succession, crisis, and incompetent occupants — is precisely what the Judges period lacks.

[210] Brueggemann, *Theology of the Old Testament*, 123–130.
[211] Gottwald, *Tribes of Yahweh*, 358–386.
[212] von Rad, *Old Testament Theology*, vol. 1, 334–352.

Over time, this produces institutional drift. Norms erode through neglect. Exceptions accumulate and harden into habit. Practices justified as temporary become precedent. Improvisation replaces rules. What begins as flexibility settles into incoherence. Disorder emerges gradually as dysfunction becomes normalized.

One of the book's most sobering insights is that instability requires little in the way of malice.[213] It follows readily from the absence of structures capable of resisting entropy. Judges depicts a society rich in moral language but poor in political capacity — and this is precisely the gap between the *effectual truth* names. Ritual, memory, and invocation of divine authority remain abundant even as enforcement weakens. Moral claims circulate frequently, yet they no longer shape behavior reliably. What the narrative insists on attending to is not what Israel believes or aspires to but what its institutional arrangements actually produce.

This disjunction between language and capacity stands among the narrative's most instructive features. Societies can retain moral vocabulary long after the institutions that once sustained it have weakened. The words remain. The mechanisms fade. Moral language shifts from formative to reactive, expressing regret where it once governed conduct.

Judges frames this condition as a structural problem. A community without consolidated authority, enforceable law, and durable institutions struggles to sustain order regardless of the sincerity of its ideals.[214] Repeated deliverance fails to produce lasting reform because deliverance is itself the problem: each judge is a response to *necessità* that leaves the conditions producing necessity unchanged. Moral exhortation lacks the capacity to substitute for political structure, and charismatic leadership cannot resolve systemic weakness — it can only manage its symptoms until the next crisis arrives.

The narrative therefore moves toward the demand for kingship. The request centers on continuity, enforcement, and coordination — authority that persists beyond emergency. Judges prepares the reader to see why centralized rule appears as political necessity, not betrayal of ideals.

---

[213] Berger, *Sacred Canopy*, 21–28.

[214] Childs, *Introduction to OT as Scripture*, 255–262.

Judges is not a preview of Machiavelli. It is political analysis conducted in narrative form, using the same diagnostic logic: begin with what arrangements actually produce, not with what they aspire to; attend to the gap between moral language and institutional capacity; identify the recurring patterns that emerge when *necessità* governs without structural response. The book's conclusion — the demand for kingship — is not a theological capitulation but a political judgment: that *virtù* without office, authority without continuity, and leadership without institutional form cannot sustain order across generations regardless of the sincerity of the ideals involved.

Judges thus stands as a case study in political fragility. It exposes the limits of moral aspiration when detached from institutional form. It demonstrates how communities can know the law, affirm the good, and still fail to govern themselves effectively. Disorder emerges less from ignorance or malice than from arrangements unable to sustain coherence over time.

Read in this way, Judges becomes an anatomy of instability: a sustained examination of what happens when moral vision outpaces institutional design — and when the only answer a political community has learned to give to the problem of necessity is to produce another judge.

CHAPTER 18

KINGSHIP AND CONSOLIDATION

The biblical books of Samuel and Kings record Israel's transition from a loose tribal confederation into a centralized monarchy.[215] Among the problems of political life, none occupied Machiavelli more persistently than this one: what does it cost to find durable order, and how should that cost be judged? His answer — that founders are evaluated not by the means they used but by the endurance of what they built, and that the violence inseparable from founding is a different moral category from the cruelty of ordinary governance — runs through *The Prince* from beginning to end. Samuel and Kings present the same problem in narrative form, with the same unflinching attention to what consolidation actually requires.

These texts read as political history rendered in narrative form. Alongside questions of covenant and worship, they attend closely to taxation, military organization, succession, courts, and the problem of coordinating a people over time. They trace the emergence of permanent office, the construction of a standing apparatus of rule, and sustained disagreement over the purpose and limits of kingship.

This chapter examines that transition as an institutional response to instability. Judges unfolds through recurring emergencies: moments in which crisis produces leadership, order is briefly restored, and authority dissolves back into local autonomy. Kingship begins when that pattern proves inadequate — when *necessità* becomes chronic enough that the community recognizes it cannot go on governing by emergency alone. What follows is what Machiavelli calls the founding moment: the conversion of survival from improvisation into permanence, which requires not just a capable leader but an institutional architecture capable of persisting after the leader is gone.

The biblical narrative treats this shift with unusual candor — the same candor Machiavelli insists political analysis requires. Centralization stabilizes law and defense while concentrating power, regularizing extraction, and hardening

215 Lemche, *Early Israel*, 1–30; Römer, *Deuteronomistic History*, 1–35.

hierarchy. A king coordinates what tribes cannot, and the same machinery that protects also imposes burden. Capacity gained through consolidation narrows freedom through obligation. This is not presented as corruption or betrayal. It is presented as the structural truth of political founding: order costs something, and the cost is borne by those who are ordered.

Where Judges exposes the dangers of fragmentation, kingship reveals the logic of consolidation. The move from tribal coalition to monarchy reorganizes authority, obligation, and continuity across collective life. Leadership ceases to depend on episodic crisis and becomes embedded in office. Authority acquires duration.

The demand for a king arises from *necessità* in the precise sense Machiavelli gives that term: not merely a practical problem but a structural constraint that forecloses the alternatives.[216] External threats intensify. Internal disorder persists. Decentralized leadership struggles to sustain security across generations. Emergency solutions prove insufficient. Charismatic deliverers succeed briefly and vanish without leaving durable structure behind. Each cycle reinforces the same lesson: improvisation cannot substitute for governance. The founding moment arrives not when the people desire a king but when continued fragmentation becomes existentially untenable.

The society therefore confronts a hard choice centered on survivability. The request for a king reflects recognition of systemic inadequacy, not desire for domination. Moral unity without political unity cannot endure under pressure. Shared identity, unsupported by continuous authority, fails to organize defense, enforce law, or stabilize expectation.

Kingship promises unity of command, continuity of authority, and the capacity for coordinated action across time and territory.[217] Authority becomes enduring. Leadership embeds itself in office, not crisis. Decisions issued from a central source with ongoing jurisdiction. Expectations stabilize. Precedent accumulates. Authority persists beyond the lifespan, charisma, or competence of any single ruler.

---

[216] Brueggemann, *First and Second Samuel*, 60–74.

[217] von Rad, *Old Testament Theology*, vol. 1, 344–352.

A loose network of overlapping loyalties reorganizes into hierarchy. The political system acquires memory. Procedures emerge. Roles become predictable. Governance shifts from reaction toward administration. Power becomes ordinary instead of exceptional. Authority moves from episodic to structural.

Consolidation enables scale. Defense can be planned. Military forces standardize training and deployment.[218] Logistics replace heroism. Victory becomes a function of organization, not contingency — which is precisely Machiavelli's argument about military capacity as a political institution. A state that commands its own arms governs itself; a state whose survival depends on contingency, on the heroism of an individual judge appearing at the right moment, remains perpetually exposed. Law extends beyond local boundaries, disputes are adjudicated within shared frameworks, and uniform standards replace regional custom. Conflict persists, but it is processed through institutions instead of through *fortuna*.

Consolidation converts vulnerability into capacity — and this is the standard by which Machiavelli evaluates founders. His question is not whether the means used to establish order were morally clean but whether the order established was durable. Moses, Romulus, Cyrus: these are his exemplary founders, each of whom used force, deception, or coercion in the founding moment and each of whom is judged not by those means but by what endured afterward. Samuel and Kings present the same evaluative logic. The question the narrative asks of Saul and David is not whether they were righteous men but whether the institutions they built could carry the political community beyond their own lifespans.

Consolidation also demands resources, and the biblical narrative names them directly. Samuel's warning speech to the people — that a king will take their sons for his armies, their daughters for his household, their fields and vineyards for his officials, a tenth of everything they produce — is not a theological objection to kingship.[219] It is a political inventory of founding costs. Kingship transforms sporadic contribution into permanent obligation. Taxation becomes institutionalized. Labor is organized. Military service regularizes. Administrative functions expand to manage extraction and enforcement. Samuel describes what Machiavelli would later call the structural truth of founding: that the apparatus of

---

[218] Miller, *History of Ancient Israel*, 141–158.

[219] Tsumura, *First Book of Samuel*; Westbrook, *Studies in Biblical and Cuneiform Law*, 15–36.

durable order must be built from something, and that something is extracted from the people who will be ordered.

The biblical text presents these trade-offs directly, but Machiavelli takes the analysis of this consolidation a step further by looking directly at its greatest architect: King David.[220] As Leo Strauss observes, Machiavelli deliberately places the godly king in the category of tyrants, noting that his foundational acts were "most cruel and inimical" not only to Christian life, but to every humane manner of living. To illustrate the effectual truth of this reign, Machiavelli executes a brilliant subversion of the tradition's own moral language. When describing David's ruthless policy of making the rich poor and the poor rich, he directly quotes the New Testament's *Magnificat*. By applying words of divine praise to the brutal political reordering required of a new prince, Machiavelli implies that the Biblical God Himself operates with the tyrannical necessity required of all true founders.

This consolidation, however, introduces a new structural vulnerability. David succeeded because he possessed his own arms, vanquishing his neighbors through martial virtue instead of relying on chance or the arms of others.[221] Yet the very institutionalization of his power bred complacency. Machiavelli tacitly contrasts David's armed founding with the era of his successor, Solomon, noting that David's successors were ultimately "weak princes". The machinery of kingship stabilizes authority so that it outlasts the charismatic founder, but the peace it secures inevitably erodes the virtue that built it. Monarchy functions as a structural response to political fragmentation, but it does not escape the decay inherent in all human things.

This transformation reshapes the relationship between individual and polity. Participation no longer depends on enthusiasm or immediate threat. It operates through compulsion by design. Autonomy narrows. Local discretion yields to centralized command. Hierarchies harden. Distance grows between ruler and ruled. Governance gains capacity and loses intimacy. The political community becomes more resilient and more stratified.

---

220 Strauss, *Thoughts on Machiavelli*, 48–49.

221 Strauss, *Thoughts on Machiavelli*, 183–84.

The biblical text presents these trade-offs directly, in the same posture Machiavelli brings to his founding analysis: description without consolation, attention to what founding actually produces, not to what it claims.[222] Kingship delivers stability and imposes burden. It enables collective survival and restricts individual freedom. It protects against external domination and enforces internal discipline. The warning that a king will take — resources, labor, loyalty — describes a structural feature of consolidation, not a moral aberration. Machiavelli's point is identical: the violence and extraction inseparable from founding are not evidence that the founding was unjust, but evidence that durable order is not free.

This candor reflects political sophistication. Order carries cost. Legitimacy requires administration. Administration requires funding, staffing, and enforcement. Authority that governs continuously extracts continuously.

From this transition emerges a general political sequence extending beyond the biblical case. Durable order depends on administration.[223] Administration depends on authority. Authority depends on enforcement. Enforcement depends on resources. Political unity remains fragile without institutions capable of acting continuously across time.

Machiavelli articulates this logic in its starkest form in his analysis of the *principe nuovo* — the new prince who must found order, not inherit it.[224] The new prince cannot rely on custom, hereditary legitimacy, or the expectations that stabilize established regimes. He must create those expectations, which requires acting in ways that established moral norms would otherwise condemn. States that refuse to acknowledge what founding costs preserve weakness, not purity; their independence becomes symbolic while their vulnerability becomes material. Samuel and Kings arrive at the same conclusion through narrative instead of argument. The choice to accept a king is not a betrayal of the covenant. It is the recognition that the covenant requires a political form capable of enduring, and that endurance has a price.

---

[222] Gordon, *1 & 2 Samuel*, 109–118.
[223] Walzer, *In God's Shadow*, 83–102.
[224] Machiavelli, *The Prince*, chs. 6–8; Skinner, *Foundations*, 130–141.

Kingship therefore marks a transformation of communal life. What diminishes in spontaneity grows in endurance. What contracts in local autonomy expands in collective security. Monarchy functions as a structural response to political problems, not a moral resolution. The alternative to consolidation remains exposure — to invasion, fragmentation, and perpetual emergency.

Decentralized systems preserve certain forms of independence at the cost of chronic instability. They endure by circumstance, not design. Judges records the cost of that dependence. The turn to kingship reflects a willingness to exchange improvisation for structure and vulnerability for coordination.

◆

The biblical narrative presents this choice without illusion. Kingship arises because the existing order cannot hold.[225] Consolidation becomes the price of survival. Monarchy seeks to give moral vision institutional form.

Its success depends on how authority is exercised, restrained, and renewed. But the founding question — the one Machiavelli returns to repeatedly and the one Samuel and Kings frame with equal directness — is prior to those questions of exercise and restraint. Before asking whether a king governed well, the narrative asks whether a king could be built at all from the material available, under the conditions that actually obtained, at the cost that founding actually demanded. Consolidation provides the vessel within which justice may be pursued. Political order advances through structures capable of carrying it across generations.

Kingship marks the moment when the moral community confronts political reality and chooses endurance over improvisation — when survival becomes a system instead of a hope. That choice is evaluated, in Samuel and Kings as in Machiavelli, not by whether the means were pure but by whether what was founded could stand.

[225] O'Donovan, *Desire of the Nations*, 148–151.

CHAPTER 19

THE MACCABEAN REVOLT

The standard account of the Maccabean revolt runs as follows: a foreign empire imposed pagan worship on faithful Jews, a priestly family rose in armed resistance, and the temple was restored. The Books of the Maccabees preserve this narrative, and it is not wrong.[226] But it is incomplete in ways that matter for the argument of this book.

The revolt was not a collision between an alien culture and an indigenous one. It was the climax of a century-long process in which Greek institutional forms had already penetrated Jewish society from within. Modern scholarship, particularly the work of Martin Hengel and Lester Grabbe, has reconstructed this process in detail that the Maccabean texts themselves deliberately obscure.[227]

Hengel's central argument is that by the time of Antiochus IV's persecution in the 160s BCE, Palestine had already been substantially shaped by Hellenistic culture through 150 years of Ptolemaic and early Seleucid rule.[228] Greek language, administrative structures, economic practices, and intellectual categories had become part of the operating environment of Jewish elites.

The crisis under Antiochus was not the first encounter between Judaism and Hellenism; it was the point at which a long accommodation turned violent. Grabbe's correction is important: the archaeological evidence does not support thorough Hellenization of Judaea before the mid-second century, and resistance to Greek rule should not be confused with resistance to Greek culture.

Jewish apocalyptic literature was part of a broader Near Eastern pattern — Egyptians, Babylonians, and Persians all produced similar resistance writings under Hellenistic domination. The Jews were not uniquely incompatible with

---

[226] Josephus, Antiquities of the Jews, 12.1–7; Lester L. Grabbe, A History of the Jews and Judaism in the Second Temple Period, vol. 2 (London: T&T Clark, 2008), 260–278.
[227] Daniel R. Schwartz, 2 Maccabees (Berlin: De Gruyter, 2008), 1–45; Martin Hengel, Judaism and Hellenism, vol. 1 (Philadelphia: Fortress, 1974), 1–32.
[228] Hengel, Judaism and Hellenism, 1:252–309. Hengel's claim that "from about the middle of the third century BC all Judaism must really be designated 'Hellenistic Judaism'" (1:104) remains the field's most provocative formulation of the thesis.

Greek civilization.[229] What made the Maccabean crisis distinctive was not cultural incompatibility but institutional capture.

The revolt's origins lie in a factional struggle within the Jerusalem aristocracy. A reform party, operating through the institutional authority of the high priesthood, sought to transform Jerusalem into a Greek *polis*.

Jason secured the high priesthood by offering Antiochus IV increased tribute and proceeded to establish a gymnasium, enroll Jerusalem's elite as citizens of a reconstituted city, and restructure the community's legal and cultural identity from the top down.[230] Menelaus outbid him and pushed the program further, alienating even moderate reformers. The critical point is that the Hellenizers did not attack the institution from outside. They occupied it from within and used its authority to redefine what the institution meant. Machiavelli has a precise name for this: it is the capture of moral language by factional interests — the specific failure mode he diagnoses across the *Discourses* and the *Florentine Histories*, where institutions designed to mediate conflict are seized by parties who use their legitimating power to advance sectional goals.

This factional context is what *1 Maccabees* as a political text works to conceal. The book is a Hasmonean legitimation narrative, composed to justify a dynasty that had seized both kingship and high priesthood — offices the Torah assigned to different lineages.[231] Its heroic resistance story simplifies a messy civil war into a clean account of righteous violence against foreign sacrilege. It performs the function Machiavelli describes founding narratives as performing: retroactive justification of the order that violence produced.

[229] Grabbe, *Second Temple Period*, 2:125–165, esp. 148: "there is really very little archaeological support for the contention that Judaea was thoroughly Hellenized before the middle of the second century BCE." Grabbe's chapter on "Hellenism and Jewish Identity" provides the most balanced assessment of the Hengel debate.

[230] 1 Macc 1:11–15; 2 Macc 4:7–17. On the reform party and the internal dynamics, see Shaye J. D. Cohen, *From the Maccabees to the Mishnah* (Louisville: Westminster John Knox, 2006), 17–34; Hengel, *Judaism and Hellenism*, 1:277–284.

[231] On 1 Maccabees as Hasmonean court history, see Schwartz, *2 Maccabees*, 11–15; Grabbe, *Second Temple Period*, 2:287–291.

The historical reconstruction reveals what the text deliberately obscures: the revolt was also an internal conflict between competing visions of what Judaism was, fought through and over the institution of the high priesthood. *Second Maccabees*, with its emphasis on martyrdom, temple theology, and divine intervention, offers a different political theology of the same events — one less concerned with dynastic legitimation and more with the question of how sacred order persists under conditions of radical coercion.[232]

◆

When Mattathias tears down the pagan altar at Modein and kills the apostate Jew who approaches it, he is Machiavelli's armed prophet. The scene in *1 Maccabees* 2 mirrors the logic of Exodus 32: sacred obligation backed by organized violence at the moment when persuasion has failed and the institutional order is collapsing.[233]

Judas Maccabeus succeeds because he commands his own arms, organizes disciplined forces, and translates moral commitment into military capacity — the precise combination Machiavelli treats as the prerequisite of durable political achievement. But the Maccabean case adds a dimension that the Moses analysis does not contain. Moses founded a new order. The Maccabees claim to restore an old one. Machiavelli's framework treats these as structurally different problems. Founders create institutions that will outlast them. Restorers inherit institutions that have been damaged and must decide how much of the old order can be recovered and how much must be rebuilt. The distance between the two is where the political problems accumulate.

The Hasmonean outcome is the effectual truth of restoration. The dynasty that fought Hellenization became a Hellenistic kingdom. Grabbe's evidence is unambiguous: Judaea under Hasmonean rule adopted Greek administrative structures, minted coins with Greek inscriptions, expanded through military

---

232 2 Macc 6–7; Schwartz, *2 Maccabees*, 63–89.

233 1 Macc 2:15–28. On the armed prophet as a Machiavellian category, see the analysis of Exodus 32 in Chapter 16 above. Cf. Machiavelli, *The Prince*, ch. 6.

conquest in ways indistinguishable from any Seleucid successor state, and made no attempt to eliminate the overt Greek elements in Palestinian culture.[234]

The moral language of resistance — covenant-fidelity, Torah-loyalty, temple-restoration — continued to operate as the legitimating vocabulary of the regime, but the institutional reality it described had been transformed. The "restored" order was a new order wearing the old order's clothes. This is the gap between aspiration and operation that Machiavelli teaches the reader to see, and it appears here with particular clarity because the Maccabean narrative itself insists so forcefully that the gap does not exist. The text's silence about what the Hasmonean state actually became is as diagnostic as what it says about what the revolt intended.

◆

The Maccabean moment thus occupies a specific position in the Part V sequence. Judges shows what happens when moral aspiration operates without institutional enforcement. Kingship shows what consolidation costs and what it produces. The Maccabean revolt shows what happens when the institution itself is captured — first by internal reformers who use its authority to transform its meaning, then by armed resisters who reclaim it in the name of restoration, and finally by the dynasty that inherits it and reproduces, under sacred language, the very structures it overthrew.

What Paul will construct in the next chapter — authority without coercion, obedience through formation, legitimacy embedded in conscience — becomes intelligible only against this background of institutional capture, armed recovery, and the permanent distance between what political orders claim and what they are.

[234] Grabbe, *Second Temple Period*, 2:149–150: the Hasmonean state "threw off the Seleucid yoke but made no attempt to eliminate the overt Greek elements in Palestinian culture" and "was typical of Hellenistic kingdoms of that general period." See also Cohen, *From the Maccabees to the Mishnah*, 36–44.

CHAPTER 20

Paul and the Architecture of Authority

Paul appears in the New Testament as an actor operating fully inside an imperial world. His life unfolds along Roman roads, within patronage networks, household hierarchies[235], synagogues, courts, and systems of surveillance and punishment. Any serious reading of Paul therefore attends to both proclamation and condition: theology articulated under constraint, mission conducted within structures shaped by imperial power.

This chapter isolates a governance-relevant dimension of Pauline life and writing: the construction of communities capable of coherence, discipline, and continuity without territory, police power, or formal sovereignty.[236] The focus is institutional clarity — how moral and spiritual claims stabilize collective life, and how durable authority emerges when external power remains indifferent or hostile.

As canonical scripture, Paul's letters have long sustained devotional and theological interpretation. Read through an institutional lens, they also disclose the mechanisms by which authority is assembled, exercised, and maintained. The question here concerns what kind of authority is being built, by what means, and with what political consequences.

Paul's letters — among the earliest Christian texts — function as governance documents for small communities attempting to endure without protection.[237] They address conflict, sexual conduct, money, leadership, discipline, dispute resolution, hierarchy, and loyalty under pressure. They respond to recurring problems: factions forming, norms eroding, authority being challenged, belief weakening under persecution. Authority appears here in the process of construction, assembled in real time without an army, territory, or state apparatus.

---

[235] Meeks, *The First Urban Christians* (New Haven: Yale University Press, 1983), 1–13.

[236] Meeks, *The First Urban Christians*. 84-85.

[237] Brown, *An Introduction to the New Testament* (New York: Doubleday, 1997).

Paul occupies a pivotal position in this sequence of institutional forms. The Maccabean revolt shows legitimacy mobilized through organized violence under existential threat. Paul demonstrates a different configuration: legitimacy reorganized so that violence recedes from the center. Rather than contesting Rome through revolt, he builds forms of order capable of operating beneath existing regimes — portable, reproducible, and internally regulated. Authority shifts from visible enforcement toward formation: shared identity, moral expectation, ritual belonging, and continuous instruction.

The political consequence is an architecture of authority oriented toward endurance. Paul supplies a model of cohesion without territorial control: hierarchy without police, discipline without routine coercion, allegiance that coexists with outward compliance while extending deeper than it. In this sense, Paul functions less as a doctrinal endpoint than as an institutional hinge — the moment when survival through episodic force gives way to endurance through internalized normativity, helping set the conditions for what will later become Christendom.

Paul's biography sharpens this insight. He enters history as an agent of repression, acting with legal sanction and moral certainty.[238] Before his conversion, he participated directly in the persecution of Christians, including arrest and death. The violence he administers is disciplined, justified, and institutionally authorized. He acts as a functionary of order, charged with enforcement and obedience.

This background matters politically. Paul understands coercion from the inside. He has exercised authority through surveillance, punishment, and lethal force. His legitimacy is inherited, his task enforcement, his loyalty directed upward through institutional command.

His conversion marks a reconfiguration of how order is sustained.[239] His seriousness about discipline, obedience, and communal coherence remains intact, while the mechanism through which these ends are achieved changes

[238] Gal 1:13–14; Phil 3:5–6; Acts 8–9; Brown, *Introduction to NT*, 423–428.

[239] Wright, *Paul and the Faithfulness of God*, 848–852.

fundamentally. The figure who once enforced belief through violence becomes the architect of a system in which violence recedes from everyday governance.

After his conversion, Paul builds communities capable of persisting within imperial rule without being absorbed by it. These communities are morally demanding, tightly regulated, and structurally coherent.[240] Authority remains central, but its location changes. It relocates from external enforcement to internal obligation.

This relocation proves decisive. Obedience shifts from fear of punishment toward conscience, identity, and shared narrative.[241] Law is reframed within formation, not abolished. Authority becomes largely self-administering, embedded in habit and expectation instead of imposed through constant coercion.

From a political perspective, this represents a major innovation. Populations that govern themselves require fewer instruments of force. Communities bound by internalized norms can endure without sovereignty, territory, or armies. Paul's churches are not states, yet they display capacities that states often struggle to maintain: cohesion without force, loyalty without surveillance, discipline without continuous enforcement.

Hierarchy remains integral. Paul establishes roles, offices, and lines of responsibility. Elders oversee conduct.[242] Deviance is corrected. Members are disciplined through rebuke, exclusion, and communal pressure. Authority operates continuously, though without the machinery of violence that characterized Paul's earlier role as persecutor.

Formation stands at the center of this system. Paul devotes sustained attention to shaping belief, habit, and identity.[243] Letters instruct behavior. Narratives interpret suffering. Rituals reinforce belonging. Language reorders status.

---

[240] Meeks, *First Urban Christians*, 84–85; 1 Cor 5–7.

[241] Barclay, *Paul and the Gift*, 3.2.

[242] Brown, *Introduction to NT*.

[243] Meeks, *First Urban Christians*, 84–110; Hurtado, *Lord Jesus Christ*, 137–143.

Individuals learn what to obey, and who they are. Obedience flows from identification, not fear.

This form of power unfolds more slowly than coercion, yet it proves far more durable. It survives persecution because it does not depend on institutions easily dismantled. It spreads laterally through imitation and testimony, not vertically through command. Where armed resistance demands constant readiness for violence, Pauline communities persist through continuity of practice.

Paul addresses authority explicitly. He instructs followers on order, restraint, and obedience. He counsels restraint in confrontation with governing powers, orienting communities toward endurance, not immediate victory.[244] By decoupling obedience from sovereignty, he enables collective life to persist under hostile regimes without perpetual escalation.

The result is a dual structure of allegiance. Outward compliance with existing authorities coexists with a deeper, internalized loyalty that transcends them.[245] Power multiplies in this arrangement. Authority becomes harder to detect and harder to destroy because it no longer depends on centralized force.

The contrast with Paul's earlier life clarifies this logic. He understands coercion intimately. He has wielded it and observed its limits. His movement away from violence reflects institutional learning, not idealism. Belief enforced through fear proves fragile; belief formed through identity reproduces itself.

Taken together, these cases trace a progression in the organization of authority. Judges reveals instability without structure. Kingship reveals the costs of consolidation.[246] The Maccabean revolt reveals resistance when legitimacy is annihilated. Paul reveals endurance through formation.

Power reorganizes; it does not vanish. Authority becomes less visible and more pervasive. Obedience becomes habitual, not episodic. Legitimacy migrates inward, embedding itself in conscience and practice. This form of power resists disruption because it feels chosen, not imposed.

---

[244] Hays, *Moral Vision of NT*, 325–342; Gaventa, *When in Romans*.
[245] Wright, *Paul and the Faithfulness of God*, 129–135; Gorman, *Reading Paul*.
[246] O'Donovan, *Desire of the Nations*, 57-58.

Machiavelli would later recognize the strength of this arrangement, stripped of theological framing. His attention to religion, habit, reputation, and belief reflects awareness that authority sustained internally outlasts authority sustained by force.[247] Paul supplies an early demonstration of this logic.

Paul's significance here is structural. He shows how authority survives without sovereignty, how obedience stabilizes without continuous violence, and how legitimacy is cultivated through formation.[248] These are the mechanisms Christendom will later inherit, formalize, and scale.

The movement from persecutor to architect marks a political innovation. Power adapts; it does not disappear. Governance migrates from the sword to formation, from coercion to conscience.

With Paul, the political anthropology traced in this book reaches its turning point. Violence yields to discipline. Survival yields to endurance.[249] Christendom represents the attempt to fuse this internalized authority with external governance, producing institutions capable of ruling entire societies while retaining moral legitimacy.

The consequences of that fusion come next.

---

[247] Machiavelli, *The Prince*, chs. 6, 15–18; Skinner, *Foundations*, 130–132.
[248] Brown, *Rise of Western Christendom*, 49.
[249] Brown, *Rise of Western Christendom*, 102–134; Berman, *Law and Revolution*, 85–119.

PART VI
FROM CHRISTENDOM TO NOW

The preceding five parts have described a civilization and the analyst who saw it most clearly.

Part I established that Machiavelli was formed by Christendom, not merely placed within it — that his analytical vocabulary, his rhetorical training, and his political problems were Christian institutional products before they were anything else.

Parts II through IV traced the specific architecture of that civilization under stress: the structural pluralism of competing authorities, the constitutional emergency when the adjudicative center failed, the machinery of office, necessity, indirect rule, reputation, and faction that governance depended on, and the limits that coercion and rival loyalties imposed on every system's durability.

Part V showed these same problems working through the specific biblical narratives that Christendom's political imagination was trained on. The reader who has followed the argument to this point now holds a precise picture of how a moralized civilization governed itself, sustained authority, managed failure, and produced the institutional forms that outlasted it.

Part VI asks what to do with that picture.

The answer the part proposes is not primarily historical. It is practical and present. Christendom's institutional legacy did not end when its theological unity fractured. The university, legal due process, corporate personhood, the political category of conscience, and the model of professional ethics — named concretely in Chapter 20 — migrated into modernity as functional forms, carrying their operating logic into new symbolic frames.[250]

The governance mechanisms traced in Parts III and IV migrated with them: authority still requires justification; obedience still requires meaning; conflict still requires channels; crisis still concentrates decision; formation still governs

[250] Gregory, *Unintended Reformation*, 365–398; Berman, *Law and Revolution*, 85–119.

behavior more pervasively than enforcement. These are Christendom's solutions to Christendom's problems, still operating — in the diocese, the Jesuit university, the NGO, the government agency, the parish — under names and justifications that have changed while the underlying mechanics have not. The reader who understands this is not reading ancient history. They are reading a description of the institutional world they currently inhabit.

Part VI is the practical payoff of the book delivered over four chapters:

Chapter 20 identifies the specific institutions Christendom built and names them by their modern descendants — showing not that there is a general continuity between medieval and modern governance but that there are five traceable, nameable institutional lines running from canon lawyers and cathedral schools directly into the operating logic of contemporary universities, courts, corporations, professional ethics systems, and constitutional rights frameworks.

Chapter 21 explains the mechanism: secularization is re-labeling and re-anchoring — the symbolic vocabulary changes while the governance function persists, and four institutional illustrations show the mechanism operating in specific, recognizable form.

Chapter 22 applies the book's full analytical framework to four institutional contexts the reader will actually inhabit — parish, Catholic university, international NGO, government agency — and supplies five diagnostic questions that can be carried into any institution anywhere.

Chapter 23 restates the book's governing thesis at full weight, develops the four ethical implications for those entering institutional leadership, and closes with a meditation on what it means to seek the good inside institutions you did not design and cannot fully control.

The animating question underneath all four chapters is the one the book has been building toward since Part I: the reader now holds both the civilization and the analyst who diagnosed it — what does that doubled perspective mean for the institutions the reader actually inhabits?

Modern institutions are Christendom's institutional legacy operating with secular labels. Machiavelli's diagnostic vocabulary — *virtù*, *fortuna*, *necessità*, the *effectual truth* — was developed inside that legacy, by a formed participant who understood its failures with the clarity that only intimacy produces. The reader who has followed this book to its final part now has access to that clarity. Part VI shows what to do with it.

CHAPTER 21

How Christendom Built Durable Institutions

I. The Architecture of Fragmented Rule

European Christendom built its institutions in a fragmented political field. Overlapping jurisdictions, competing claims to obedience[251], and the lack of an uncontested center of authority defined the landscape. Papal, imperial, royal, urban, noble, and monastic powers coexisted, clashed, and negotiated in the same space. Authority was layered, rivalrous, and often ambiguous.

Fragmentation shaped institutional development at every level. A thirteenth-century French baron owed obedience to his king, his bishop, his feudal lord, and — in matters of marriage and heresy — to Rome. Each authority could make enforceable claims on him, and none could silence the others. Governance operated in this environment of competing commands, and durable rule depended on techniques for coordination across rival authorities. Endurance came through managed plurality, not unified command.

The defining challenge was fragmentation at scale. Territories expanded, populations grew, and economic life intensified while authority remained divided. Rulers relied less on personal presence, charisma, or inherited loyalty and more on mechanisms that could operate across jurisdictions only partly under their control. Governance evolved through negotiated administration: offices, procedures, and routines capable of functioning amid competing claims.

Administration developed as a practical response to divided rule. Offices carried recurring functions beyond the reach of any single ruler.[252] Records stabilized claims in environments of dispute. Written procedures allowed decisions to persist beyond individual lifespans and circulate across institutional boundaries. Rivalry continued, yet it became governable.

[251] Strayer, *Medieval Origins*, 9–34; Tierney, *Crisis of Church and State*, 1–20.
[252] Clanchy, *From Memory to Written Record*, 116-117.

This administrative turn altered political power while leaving core tensions in place. Authority grew more impersonal and continuous even as sovereignty stayed contested. Institutions acquired memory while control remained dispersed. Precedent, delegation, and negotiated compliance increasingly replaced reliance on proclamation alone. Power flowed through function as much as through presence.

Legal systems evolved along the same logic. Europe layered norms instead of unifying law.[253] Canon law, civil law, royal law, municipal statutes, and customary practice overlapped and competed. Jurisdictional conflict became a constant feature of rule, and it generated legal sophistication, not paralysis. Courts defined competence. Appeals structured escalation. Legal reasoning became a method for managing authority amid conflict.

Moral language supplied law with legitimacy where enforcement varied. Concepts such as justice, duty, order, conscience, and obligation rendered obedience intelligible across divided rule. Law translated command into justification. Compliance rested on recognizability as well as force.

Fiscal institutions followed a similar path. Taxation often entered political life through extraordinary necessity[254] — war, defense, crisis — before settling into routine extraction. Overlapping claims provoked negotiation, exemption, and resistance. Accounting practices, fiscal offices, and standardized records emerged to stabilize these tensions. Extraction stayed contested, yet it became predictable enough to sustain institutions over time.

Discipline extended governance into everyday life through routine practice. Military organizations embedded violence within command structures. Urban regulations ordered markets, labor, and movement. A Florentine guild master in 1400 submitted to inspection schedules, quality standards, and dispute procedures without thinking of them as governance — they were simply how his trade worked. Educational and ecclesiastical institutions trained individuals to operate inside these procedural systems. Authority became ambient, exercised through routine, not spectacle.

---

[253] Berman, *Law and Revolution*, 120–126; Bellomo, *Common Legal Past of Europe*.

[254] Tilly, *Coercion, Capital*, 67–95; Bonney, *Rise of Fiscal State*, 1–44.

Professional management grew from this layered environment. Clerks, jurists, accountants, diplomats, and military officers built careers on specialized skill because rulers governed through dependence as much as command. A capable chancellor could serve two kings in succession — the office needed him more than he needed any particular patron. Skill became portable across borders. Offices outlasted the people who held them. Functions survived even when rulers fell.

Institutional growth remained uneven and crisis-driven. Wars disrupted continuity. Plague reduced administrative capacity. Reforms followed breakdowns. Innovations addressed immediate problems and persisted when useful. Redundancy and inefficiency coexisted with endurance. Durability emerged through selective retention under pressure, never through comprehensive design.

Stress drove institutionalization. Rival authority forced invention. Contested sovereignty demanded technique. Governance became systemic because personal rule proved insufficient amid persistent conflict.

These developments were not unique to Christian Europe. Islamic polities, Byzantine administration, and Chinese imperial governance faced similar challenges through different configurations. Scale, legitimacy, and coordination recur across political orders.

The European Christian pathway matters here because it was Machiavelli's environment. His analysis presupposes divided authority, moralized legitimacy, and institutional improvisation.[255] Understanding how Christendom governed under these conditions clarifies what he was diagnosing — and why his insights migrate so readily across later political forms.

II. Five Institutions That Migrated

The general account above describes processes. What it produced can be named more specifically. Five institutional forms developed within Christendom's particular constraints and migrated into modernity essentially intact, carrying their operating logic into new symbolic frames.

---

[255] Fukuyama, *Origins of Political Order*, 223–320.

The University

The medieval university was an ecclesiastical institution before it was an educational one. Bologna, Paris, Oxford, Cambridge[256] — the first European universities emerged in the twelfth and thirteenth centuries as corporations under Church protection, governed by their own statutes, exempt from local secular jurisdiction, and authorized to grant degrees that carried force across Christendom regardless of where the holder traveled.

The *universitas* was not a building or a curriculum but a legal entity: a self-governing corporation of scholars with the right to make its own rules, discipline its own members, hold property, and sue in court. The degree was a license issued by the Church, valid everywhere in Latin Christendom because the Church's jurisdiction was everywhere.

What migrated into modernity was the entire organizational structure: the self-governing scholarly corporation, the system of examinations and licensed competence, the distinction between undergraduate and graduate formation, the lecture as a method of transmitting authoritative texts, and the faculty as a body with collective governance rights. When post-Reformation universities lost their direct Church connection, they retained every one of these features. The modern research university — with its tenure system, its faculty governance, its degree-granting authority, and its claim to intellectual independence from the state — is the medieval ecclesiastical corporation operating without its theological rationale.

Legal Proceduralism

Canon law — the law of the Church, systematized from the twelfth century onward — was the most sophisticated legal system in medieval Europe and the source of most of what modernity understands as due process.[257] The canonists developed the principle that no one could be condemned without being heard (*audiatur et altera pars*). They developed the distinction between accusatorial and inquisitorial procedure. They established rules for the admission of evidence, the examination of witnesses, the right of appeal, and the requirement that judicial

---

[256] Rashdall, *Universities of Europe*; Cobban, *Medieval Universities*, chaps. 1–3.

[257] Berman, *Law and Revolution*, 199-225; Pennington, *Prince and the Law*, chaps. 1–3.

decisions be reasoned and recorded. They invented the concept of legal representation — the *procurator* who could stand in for a party before a court.

These procedural innovations were developed within the Church's court system to handle the enormous volume of disputes — over marriage, inheritance, clerical discipline, heresy, and property — that canon law governed. They migrated into secular court systems across Europe not through deliberate transfer but through trained canonists and civilians who moved between ecclesiastical and royal service.

Modern procedural due process — the right to notice, to be heard, to present evidence, to appeal — is canonist procedure operating in secular courts with secular justifications.

Corporate Personhood

The legal concept that a collective body can hold rights, own property, incur debts, and be sued as a single entity — the corporation — was developed by medieval canonists and civilians. It solved a specific Christendom problem: how does a monastery own land when monks take individual vows of poverty?[258]

The answer the canonists developed was the *universitas*: the collective body as a legal person distinct from its individual members, capable of holding property, entering contracts, and persisting across generations even as its membership changed entirely.

This concept proved extraordinarily portable. By the late medieval period it had been applied to cathedral chapters, towns, guilds, and universities. By the early modern period it had been adapted for trading companies. The joint-stock corporation of the seventeenth century — the East India Company, the Dutch VOC — is the canonical corporation with its theological rationale stripped away and its commercial application extended globally.

Modern corporate law, including the legal personhood of business entities and the liability protections that flow from it, rests on a conceptual foundation built by twelfth-century Church lawyers solving a monastic property problem.

---

[258] Berman, *Law and Revolution*, 215–224; Maitland, "*Corporation Sole*," 335–354.

Conscience as a Political Category

Medieval political theology developed the concept of conscience — the internal moral faculty that binds the individual regardless of external command — into a political category with specific institutional consequences.[259]

The question of whether an unjust law binds the conscience was not a private spiritual matter. It was a jurisprudential question with direct bearing on the limits of political authority, the rights of resistance, and the conditions under which disobedience was legitimate. Canonists and theologians developed detailed accounts of when conscience could override external command, under what conditions, and with what consequences for the authority that had issued the command.

This category migrated directly into modern political thought. The Protestant insistence on the individual conscience against institutional authority — Luther's 'Here I stand' — is not an invention but an intensification of a category that already had a century of sophisticated jurisprudential development.

The modern concept of conscientious objection, the philosophical tradition of civil disobedience from Thoreau to King, and the legal concept of a right of conscience in constitutional law all draw on the political theology of the medieval conscience debate. The word *conscientia* is still doing the same work it did in the twelfth century — marking the boundary between what external authority can demand and what the internal moral faculty will not permit.

Professional Ethics

The medieval Church developed the first systematic professional ethics in European history[260], for a specific reason: it needed to govern the behavior of clergy who operated across enormous distances, under widely varying local conditions, with no possibility of central supervision of daily practice. The solution was formation — intensive training in a body of rules, cases, and principles that would govern conduct from the inside, so that the individual cleric would know how to act correctly even when no superior was watching.

---

[259] Tierney, *Liberty and Law*; Oakley, *Natural Law*.

[260] Boyle, "*Summa Confessorum*"; Tentler, *Sin and Confession*.

Confession manuals (the *summae confessorum*) provided detailed guidance on specific cases; canon law provided the framework; episcopal oversight provided accountability. The system produced something that had not previously existed: a trained professional class with internalized ethical obligations specific to their role.

This model migrated into every modern profession. The physician's ethics, the lawyer's duties of confidentiality and loyalty, the accountant's obligations of independence and accuracy, the engineer's duty to public safety — all of these are structured on the same model: intensive formation in role-specific norms, accountability to a professional body with disciplinary authority, and internalized obligations that are supposed to govern conduct even when external oversight is absent.

The distinction between a trade (which anyone can practice) and a profession (which requires formation, licensing, and ongoing accountability to a governing body) was drawn first for the clergy. Every licensed profession is a secular clergy in this structural sense.

By Machiavelli's lifetime, political power increasingly depended on institutional operation, not lineage or charisma. Administration, law, finance, military organization, and legitimacy functioned as interconnected mechanisms. Failure arose less from personal vice than from institutional misalignment.

Christendom assembled a toolkit under constraint. That toolkit outlived the theological unity that first sustained it. As symbols shifted and authority reconfigured, the mechanisms remained available — ready to be adapted, secularized, and redeployed. Modern governance emerged through inheritance of habit: techniques refined under Christendom's pressures and carried forward into new frames.

What the five institutions described above demonstrate — in concrete, nameable, traceable form — is the book's central claim: Christendom was not the background against which modernity developed but its architectural source. The university, legal proceduralism, corporate personhood, the political category of conscience, the model of professional ethics — none of these required secularization to become modern. They arrived in modernity as Christendom's direct institutional legacy, carrying their operating logic into new symbolic frames.

The Church's canon lawyers built due process; the canonists invented the corporation; the formation system of the medieval clergy became the template for every licensed profession. To understand modern governance is to understand what Christendom built. And to understand what Christendom built is to understand why Machiavelli matters: he was the first analyst to describe the machinery clearly while it was still running — to name the gap between its moral claims and its institutional operations, to trace its failure modes and its genuine achievements, and to do so from the inside, in the language the tradition had given him, with the clarity that only a formed participant can achieve.

CHAPTER 22

Secularization as Re-Labeling and Re-Anchoring

The decline of European Christendom changed the public language of governance while leaving the core governance tasks intact.[261] Authority needed justification. Obedience needed an intelligible frame. Conflict needed containment. Crisis demanded decisions that compressed ordinary limits. The change arrived first in the symbols and anchors through which these functions were carried.

Secularization can be read as a process of re-labeling and re-anchoring.[262] Explicitly theological vocabulary receded from public monopoly, while administrative technique, legitimacy production, and enforcement practice continued because they solved persistent problems. Symbols moved faster than operating constraints.

The most visible shift appeared in legitimacy language. In Christendom, authority was articulated through theological categories — grace and sin, divine order, vocation, stewardship, obedience to God. Political obligation presented itself as participation in a moral and cosmic order. Rule carried meaning alongside force.

As consensus weakened, legitimacy relocated into new vocabularies. Modern governance speaks of rights, dignity, security, welfare, equality, and public safety.[263] These terms perform similar institutional work: they justify authority, explain sacrifice, and make obedience intelligible. Law appears as protection of shared goods; compliance appears as participation in a collective project.

The continuity here is functional. Authority that cannot render itself credible becomes brittle. Moral language — religious or secular — supplies a grammar through which power becomes acceptable. Vocabulary changes; the demand for justification persists.

---

[261] Taylor, *A Secular Age*, 11-15.

[262] Cavanaugh, *Migrations of the Holy*, 1–25.

[263] Koselleck, *Futures Past*, 82–104.

A parallel shift occurred in the anchoring of institutional authority. In Christendom, authority is attached to sacrament, office, and sacred hierarchy. Bishops, priests, and ecclesiastical courts exercised power through roles believed to carry weight beyond individual occupants.

Modern institutions attach authority to different anchors: constitutions, procedure, professional expertise, credentialing, certification, and appointment. Authority presents itself as rational, neutral, and technical, no longer divinely grounded. Yet the organizational logic of the office remains. Power resides in roles more than persons. Positions outlast occupants. Decisions remain continuous, impersonal, and transferable. The anchor changes; the form persists.

What Taylor Describes and What This Account Adds

Charles Taylor's *A Secular Age* is the most sustained philosophical account of secularization in English, and any serious treatment of the subject must reckon with it.[264] Taylor argues that the shift from a naively theistic to a secular age is not best understood as the subtraction of religion from a previously religious culture — as though science simply dissolved superstition and left rational modernity behind. His argument is more subtle: what changed was the entire social imaginary within which both belief and unbelief are possible.

Medieval Christians did not choose to believe in God the way a modern person might deliberate about joining a religion. Belief was the default condition of a world in which the sacred was embedded in nature, time, and social structure. Secularization, on Taylor's account, is the long process through which that enchanted world was dismantled — partly through the Reformation's disenchantment of sacred spaces, partly through the development of exclusive humanism as a self-sufficient moral framework, partly through the buffering of the self against cosmic forces — until belief became one option among many instead of the background condition of life.

This is an account of experienced transformation — of how it felt, from the inside, to inhabit a world in which the sacred was progressively de-embedded from nature, time, and social structure. It is also, deliberately, an account of what was lost as well as what changed: the fullness of meaning available in an enchanted

[264] Taylor, *A Secular Age*; Gorski, *Disciplinary Revolution*; Casanova, *Public Religions*.

world, the porousness of the pre-modern self to spiritual forces, the sense that moral order was built into the fabric of things rather than constructed by human will.

The re-labeling account offered in this chapter operates at a different register and asks a different question. Taylor wants to know what secularization meant — how it transformed the conditions of belief and the texture of moral experience. This chapter asks what it did — how institutions adapted their operating logic as their symbolic anchors shifted. These are compatible questions, but they produce different kinds of evidence and different kinds of claims.

Taylor's evidence is philosophical, literary, and phenomenological: the poetry of Hopkins, the philosophy of Descartes, the theology of the Reform. This account's evidence is institutional and operational: what happened to the hospital, the university, the court, the professional guild, the fiscal system, when the explicitly Christian rationale that had organized them receded.

The re-labeling thesis does not dispute Taylor's claim that something profound happened to the conditions of belief. It disputes the implication — not always Taylor's explicit claim, but a common inference from his work — that understanding secularization requires primarily an account of changing social imaginaries. Social imaginaries change. Institutions adapt. The adaptation is often faster, more pragmatic, and less conscious than Taylor's account of transformed imaginaries suggests.

Canon lawyers did not experience a crisis of meaning when their procedural innovations migrated into royal courts and eventually into modern administrative law. Hospital administrators did not feel the loss of an enchanted world when the charitable institution founded by a religious order became a municipal or state institution. They made the relevant adjustments — to funding sources, to governance structures, to the language used to justify their authority — and the institution continued.

This is what the re-labeling account captures that Taylor's does not: the way governance mechanisms outlast not only the beliefs of those who built them but also the felt sense of transformation that Taylor describes so carefully. The machinery keeps running while the social imaginary shifts.

The operating constraints — the need to justify authority, contain conflict, manage succession, extract resources, discipline behavior — are indifferent to whether the people operating within them feel enchanted or disenchanted, porous or buffered. Machiavelli's analytical value, from this perspective, is precisely that he was attending to the machinery, not to the felt quality of life within it. He describes what Christendom's institutions do, not what it feels like to inhabit them — which is why his observations survive the transition from a theistic to a secular social imaginary largely intact.

Enforcement changes in presentation more than in necessity. In Christendom, punishment often appeared personal, visible, and morally explicit[265] — public correction, ritual sanction, ecclesiastical discipline, exemplary penalty — framed within a moral narrative. Modern enforcement operates through bureaucratic procedure. Police, courts, regulatory agencies, and administrative penalties run through standardized processes. Punishment becomes routine; discretion is constrained; authority travels through files, timelines, forms, and appeals more than spectacle.

This proceduralization makes coercion predictable and legible. Force appears as an endpoint, not a performance. Compliance follows expectation of consequence within a system of rules. The behavior regulated remains similar; the mode of governance becomes more administrative.

Narrative production migrates as well. In Christendom, collective meaning was organized through pulpit, liturgy, calendar, and ritual repetition.[266] Sermons interpreted events. Feast days structured time. Public ceremony embedded authority within sacred history. Modern societies perform this work through schools, media, civic rituals, commemorations, museums, legal discourse, and public education. Events are framed through national histories, humanitarian narratives, and appeals to collective identity. Crisis receives explanation, sacrifice receives justification, continuity receives a story.

[265] Foucault, *Discipline and Punish*, 145–156.

[266] Bellah, "*Civil Religion in America*," 1–21.

Narrative labor remains a governance function. Shared frames stabilize interpretation and reduce fragmentation. Theology once carried that public work; secular narrative infrastructure now carries it through different institutions and media.

Re-Labeling in Practice: Four Institutional Illustrations

The re-labeling thesis is easier to assert than to demonstrate. The following four examples illustrate the mechanism operating in specific institutional contexts — showing how the same governance function was carried first by a theological category and then by a secular one, with the institutional form largely intact throughout.

Grace → Dignity

In medieval Christian thought, grace designated the unearned divine gift that elevated human beings beyond their natural condition and grounded their claim to be treated as ends rather than merely as means.

The political consequence of the doctrine of grace was a floor on how human beings could be treated — not because of anything they had earned or produced but because of what they were in relation to God. This theological grounding sustained the Church's hospital system, its almsgiving obligations, and its periodic resistance to practices that treated human beings as purely instrumental — as property, as units of labor, as expendable material for state purposes.

The concept of human dignity in modern human rights law performs exactly this function. It designates an inviolable floor on treatment that does not depend on merit, productivity, citizenship, or any earned quality.

The 1948 Universal Declaration of Human Rights opens by grounding rights in the 'inherent dignity' of all members of the human family — a formulation that is deliberately universal and deliberately non-theological. The institutional machinery it sustains — international human rights courts, constitutional protections against degrading treatment, the prohibitions on torture that survive even wartime emergency — is the same machinery the grace doctrine sustained, operating with a secular anchor. The content of the protection is virtually identical; the justificatory vocabulary has changed entirely.

Sin → Pathology

The medicalization of deviance — the replacement of sin as the primary category for understanding wrongdoing with psychological and psychiatric categories — is one of the most studied transitions in the history of modern governance. What is less often noted is how precisely the institutional apparatus migrated.

Medieval and early modern Christian governance of deviant behavior operated through confession, penance, spiritual direction, and if necessary ecclesiastical discipline or secular punishment framed in moral terms. The sinner was responsible, the act was freely chosen, the remedy was spiritual transformation through repentance and reform.

Modern therapeutic governance operates through diagnosis, treatment, rehabilitation, and if necessary civil commitment or incarceration framed in clinical terms. The patient is understood as suffering from a condition, the act is produced by that condition, the remedy is therapeutic intervention aimed at behavioral change. The institutional apparatus — the supervised individual, the case file, the treatment plan, the graduated reintegration into society — maps almost exactly onto its penitential predecessor.

Michel Foucault noticed this continuity and found it sinister. The re-labeling account finds it unremarkable: governance functions require institutional carriers, and when the theological carrier became unavailable, a clinical carrier was developed that could perform the same functions within a secular legitimacy framework. The behavior being governed (violence, sexual deviance, dishonesty, substance use) is largely the same; the vocabulary governing it has shifted from moral to medical.

Vocation → Professional Identity

The doctrine of vocation — the Protestant and (in a different form) the Catholic insistence that ordinary work done faithfully in one's station was a form of service to God and therefore carried inherent dignity and moral seriousness — was the theological rationale for treating work as more than mere economic activity. A physician treating the sick was not just earning a living; he was fulfilling a divine calling. A teacher educating children was not just transmitting information; she was participating in the formation of souls. This gave work a moral seriousness and an ethical obligation structure that purely economic accounts of employment cannot supply.

The modern concept of professional identity and professional ethics is the secular carrier of vocation. When a physician speaks of her 'calling to medicine,' or when a lawyer describes his duty to the client as a professional obligation that overrides personal interest, they are using the structure of vocational ethics without the theological rationale that originally grounded it.

Medical ethics, legal ethics, and the ethics of every other licensed profession are organized around the claim that professional work carries obligations that are not reducible to contractual exchange — that the professional owes duties that arise from the role itself, not merely from what the client pays for. This is the vocation doctrine operating without God. The institutional form — the duty of care, the fiduciary obligation, the professional discipline system — is the ecclesiastical formation model with secular credentials.

Sacrament → Credentialing

Medieval ordination was a sacrament: a ritual act that conferred a permanent change in the ordained person's status, authorized them to exercise specific functions that others could not perform, and made their exercise of those functions valid regardless of their personal virtue.

A priest in mortal sin could still validly celebrate the Eucharist; the validity of the sacrament depended on ordination, not on personal holiness. This created a clear distinction between the person and the office — between the individual's moral character and their institutional authorization to act.

Modern credentialing performs this function with secular machinery. A physician licensed by a medical board is authorized to perform procedures that unlicensed persons cannot legally perform, regardless of whether any particular licensed physician is more skilled than any particular unlicensed one. The license is the sacrament: it confers a status that authorizes specific acts, persists independently of the individual's moral character (subject to discipline proceedings), and distinguishes the authorized practitioner from everyone else.

The bar examination, the medical boards, the CPA certification, the engineering PE license — these are ordination rites conducted by professional bodies rather than bishops, conferring the right to exercise functions reserved to the licensed regardless of the personal virtue of the licensed person. The institutional logic is identical; the theological rationale has been replaced by a regulatory one.

◆

Across the transition, familiar elements remain in view: enforcement and compliance, contested authority, fragile legitimacy, and reliance on intermediaries — professionals, educators, administrators — who translate abstract authority into daily practice. Power operates through habit, expectation, and internalized norms long before force becomes necessary.

Reading secularization as re-anchoring clarifies the kind of continuity at issue here. Institutions keep mechanisms that address recurring constraints. They replace symbolic frames when credibility erodes and adopt new justifications as older ones fracture. Governance evolves through performance under pressure more than through ideological coherence.

This is why Machiavelli remains useful at the end of this story. He trained readers to see operating constraints beneath public language. He analyzed legitimacy construction, authority concentration under necessity, reputation's role in obedience, and the ways institutions metabolize conflict. The point is to notice how quickly symbols change and how steadily structures persist — how power often endures by redescribing itself.

Secularization altered vocabulary and re-anchored authority in forms capable of surviving plural belief. The mechanics endure because the problems endure.

CHAPTER 23

Institutional Literacy for the Reader

The purpose of this book is to equip the reader to understand power as it operates. That understanding depends on institutional literacy: the capacity to read how authority functions within political, social, economic, and cultural systems, regardless of how those systems describe themselves. Institutional literacy renders power legible, not mysterious.

Institutional literacy begins with a basic recognition: power concentrates in systems.[267] It moves through connected mechanisms; it does not reside in a single person, office, or document. Leaders represent authority; mechanisms carry it. Laws articulate rules; institutions execute them. Ideals generate loyalty; structures organize behavior. Authority endures through coordinated functions more than through intention.

To understand any system — government, corporation, church, university, movement, or organization — the reader learns to identify the mechanisms that sustain it. These mechanisms operate in plain sight and fade into the background through familiarity. Routine provides cover more reliably than secrecy.

Every system rests on claims that justify its authority. These claims answer a basic question: why obey?[268] Legitimacy may draw on law, tradition, morality, ideology, expertise, religion, popular consent, or performance. Most systems combine several sources at once. Legal authority is reinforced through moral language. Technical competence is framed as responsibility. Tradition is defended as stability. These justifications operate continuously and intensify under pressure.

Legitimacy shapes the visibility of enforcement. When legitimacy is strong, compliance feels ordinary and enforcement recedes into the background. When legitimacy weakens, enforcement becomes conspicuous:[269] rules multiply,

---

[267] Weber, *Economy and Society*, 212–232.

[268] Weber, *Economy and Society*, 289–301.

[269] Beetham, *Legitimation of Power*, 15–33.

surveillance expands, penalties harden, and consequences arrive more quickly. Visible enforcement often signals a fragile justificatory base.

Reading a system therefore begins with its legitimating language. Observe how it explains its right to rule, manage, direct, or decide. Legitimacy is sustained through repetition under constraint. A system's self-description reveals where it anticipates challenge and where it senses vulnerability.

Enforcement defines the practical limits of acceptable behavior. It marks the boundary where persuasion yields to consequence. Enforcement includes laws, courts, contracts, security forces, regulatory agencies, professional discipline, financial penalties, credentialing systems, and social exclusion. Some mechanisms operate formally; others operate informally. Together, they establish the costs of deviation.

Systems disclose their priorities through enforcement patterns. Consistent enforcement stabilizes authority. Selective enforcement produces arbitrariness. Absent enforcement dissolves norms. The diagnostic question is concrete: where does disobedience become expensive, for whom, and how quickly? Which violations trigger rapid response, and which are tolerated? The answers reveal a hierarchy of values in practice.

Power rarely travels directly from leadership to population. It moves through intermediaries.[270] Administrators, managers, officials, clergy, professionals, supervisors, and local authorities translate abstract authority into lived reality. They interpret rules, apply discretion, manage exceptions, and absorb blame. They form the operational core of governance.

Public narratives often focus on leaders, institutions, or ideals. Outcomes depend on how intermediaries implement, delay, soften, intensify, or quietly ignore policy. Power becomes practical at this level. Institutional literacy therefore locates the handoff points where decisions turn into action.

Alongside enforcement, systems require meaning. Narrative organizes perception before action occurs. Every system produces explanations for success and failure, reward and punishment, obedience and dissent. These narratives

---

[270] Lipsky, *Street-Level Bureaucracy*, 3–11.

frame suffering as necessary, outcomes as inevitable, and authority as reasonable. They instruct people how to interpret what happens to them.

In Christendom, this work was carried by sermons, rituals, calendars, and symbolic order. In modern systems, it is carried by schools, media, professional language, policy framing, institutional messaging, and historical narrative. The medium differs; the function persists. Authority depends on interpretive coherence. When events lose shared meaning, order destabilizes and resistance becomes more likely.

Narrative stabilizes by limiting interpretive chaos and channeling dissent into recognizable forms. It designates what counts as normal, necessary, and unavoidable. Reading a system therefore requires attention to the categories it uses to explain disruption and justify continuity.

Durable systems also develop channels for dissent. Courts, elections, petitions, unions, protests, media, grievance procedures, committees, and review boards absorb pressure and convert conflict into process. These outlets allow correction without collapse.[271]

Systems become brittle when dissent loses workable channels. Pressure accumulates, grievances harden, and disagreement shifts from managed contestation into rupture. Institutional health is visible at these boundaries: which forms of dissent are tolerated, which are processed, and which are punished.

Institutional literacy produces clarity. It allows the reader to see beyond appearance, beyond moral self-description, and beyond symbolic authority to the operating architecture that governs behavior. Ideals matter within this frame because structures either sustain them or erode them. Moral aspiration without structure dissipates. Structure without legitimacy hardens. Power operates in the space between.

To read institutions clearly is to meet them with steadier attention. It reduces surprise. It increases discernment.

---

[271] Hirschman, *Exit, Voice, and Loyalty*, 30–43.

The Framework Applied: Four Institutional Contexts

The framework described above is most useful when it makes contact with specific institutions. What follows applies the diagnostic elements — legitimacy sources, enforcement patterns, intermediary structures, narrative production, and dissent channels — to four institutional contexts likely to be inhabited by this book's readers.

The Parish and Diocese

The parish is among the most studied institutions in the sociology of religion and among the least examined as a political institution in the Machiavellian sense. Applied to the parish, the diagnostic framework immediately reveals that the legitimacy sources are multiple and not always mutually reinforcing.

The parish draws on sacramental authority (the ordained priest can do what no one else can do), theological legitimacy (the teaching of the Church as received), pastoral legitimacy (the priest's personal credibility with the congregation), and institutional legitimacy (canonical standing, appointment by the bishop, membership in a diocese). These sources usually align. When they diverge — when a canonically valid but pastorally alienating priest is assigned to a congregation that trusted his predecessor — the resulting strain is diagnostic: enforcement becomes visible (Mass attendance drops, giving falls, volunteers disappear) precisely because legitimacy has weakened.

The diocese is a more complex institutional object. Diocesan authority derives from episcopal ordination, canonical law, and Rome's recognition — but is exercised through an elaborate intermediary structure of chancellors, vicar generals, pastors, deacons, and lay administrators whose discretionary interpretation of diocesan policy is where the institution's actual character is formed.

A bishop's stated priorities become diocesan reality only insofar as intermediaries implement them; a bishop's stated tolerance for dissent becomes actual policy only insofar as chancery officials communicate and model it. The diagnostic question for anyone entering diocesan service — or evaluating a diocese from outside — is not what the bishop says but what the chancellor does.

Dissent channels in the parish-diocesan system are formally limited and informally abundant. Canonically, the recourse structure runs upward through the diocese to Rome; practically, dissent operates through exit (leaving the parish or the Church), voice (organized lay advocacy, media attention, direct confrontation), and loyalty (continued presence with quiet non-compliance). The institutional health of a parish is visible in which of these is most active: a parish with high exit and low voice has foreclosed dissent instead of processing it. Faction in the parish context typically presents itself in theological or liturgical language — disputes over music, ritual style, devotional practice — while actually tracking the underlying authority dispute between competing visions of what the institution is for.

The Catholic University

Georgetown, Fordham, Loyola, Boston College, Notre Dame — the Jesuit and Catholic university is a specifically interesting institutional object because it operates with formally dual legitimacy: it claims both academic authority (derived from scholarly standards, accreditation, faculty governance, and the secular professional norms of the disciplines) and Catholic mission authority (derived from the charism of the founding order, the Church's educational tradition, and the institution's self-understanding as evangelically purposeful). These two legitimacy sources are genuinely compatible but also genuinely in tension, and how any particular institution manages that tension defines its actual institutional character more than any mission statement.

Enforcement in the Catholic university is distributed across multiple systems with different accountability structures. Academic enforcement (tenure and promotion, course approval, research ethics) operates through faculty governance and disciplinary norms that are largely independent of Catholic identity. Administrative enforcement (hiring policy, speaker approval, student conduct) is more directly shaped by institutional Catholic commitments but varies enormously across institutions.

The diagnostic question is where the two systems intersect: which violations of Catholic teaching trigger administrative response, which are handled through academic freedom norms, and which are quietly not enforced at all? The answer to that question — which is usually visible in how the institution handles contested cases in bioethics, sexuality, or political theology — reveals more about the institution's actual operating commitments than its published mission statement.

The intermediary structure of the Jesuit university is particularly complex because the Jesuit community, the lay administration, the faculty, and the board of trustees constitute four distinct authority centers with different accountability relationships. The provincials hold formal religious authority over the Jesuits; the board holds legal authority over the institution; the president navigates between them while managing the lay administration; the faculty exercises authority over curriculum and academic standards through governance structures that are largely autonomous. Institutional literacy in this context means tracking which of these centers is actually setting priorities in any given domain — and noticing when stated priority (Jesuit mission) and actual resource allocation (enrollment growth, US News rankings, donor relations) diverge.

The International NGO or Development Organization

The international NGO occupies a distinctive position in the institutional landscape because its legitimacy is explicitly non-coercive and multi-sourced. It draws on moral legitimacy (the humanitarian mission, the claim to represent the interests of beneficiaries), donor legitimacy (the authority conferred by major funders — government agencies, foundations, multilateral institutions — whose priorities shape what the organization actually does), professional legitimacy (the expertise of staff in specific technical domains), and local legitimacy (the relationships built with communities in program areas, which are often the most fragile and the most operationally consequential). These sources frequently conflict: donor priorities may not align with community needs; professional staff judgment may contradict funder requirements; moral mission may be invoked to paper over accountability failures.

Enforcement in the NGO context is primarily reputational and financial, not legal. The most powerful enforcement mechanism is donor approval, which operates through grant cycles, reporting requirements, audits, and the ability to defund. The second most powerful is media and civil society scrutiny, which can damage the reputational legitimacy on which fundraising depends. Internal enforcement through HR systems and organizational policy is formally present but operationally limited in field contexts where staff exercise wide discretion far from headquarters oversight.

The diagnostic question for anyone working in or evaluating an NGO is: whose disapproval is the organization actually managed to avoid? The answer to that question — which may be USAID, or a major foundation, or a board member with strong views, or a journalist covering the sector — identifies the real enforcement structure beneath the mission language.

Faction in the international NGO typically presents itself as a dispute over program approach (participatory vs. technical, rights-based vs. service-delivery, local ownership vs. expatriate expertise) while actually tracking a deeper contest over organizational identity and the allocation of influence between headquarters and field, between funders and implementers, between professional staff and community partners.

Dissent channels are formally present (staff surveys, management feedback processes, ethics hotlines) and practically limited because the employment relationship creates strong incentives for loyalty over voice, especially for national staff in program countries where alternative employment is scarce.

An institutionally literate participant in this context learns to read the gap between the organization's public narrative (community-driven, locally owned, participatory) and its actual authority structure (funder-driven, headquarters-controlled, expatriate-led) as the primary diagnostic indicator of institutional health.

The Political Office or Government Agency

The government agency is in some respects the institutional context for which the Machiavellian framework was originally developed, and applying it here produces the most direct connection to the book's central analytical vocabulary.

The legitimacy of a government agency derives from at least three distinct sources: legal authority (the statute or executive order that created the agency and defines its mandate), political authority (the current administration's priorities and the agency head's relationship to elected officials), and professional or technical authority (the expertise of career staff and the professional norms of the relevant domain — public health, environmental science, law enforcement, foreign policy). These three sources are in continuous negotiation, and major institutional failures typically occur when one source attempts to override the others without adequate legitimacy of its own.

Enforcement in the government agency is formal and publicly visible in ways that private institutions are not — regulations, sanctions, prosecutorial decisions, licensing actions — but the discretion exercised in enforcement is where institutional character is most clearly revealed. Which violations of the agency's mandate are pursued and which are deprioritized, which political pressures reshape enforcement priorities and which are resisted by career staff, which enforcement actions are taken in election years and which are deferred — these patterns are the effectual truth of the agency's operation, visible beneath the formal legal framework.

Machiavelli's observation that consistency of enforcement stabilizes authority while selective enforcement produces arbitrariness applies with particular force in regulatory contexts: industries that learn they can negotiate enforcement will do so, and the regulatory authority erodes in proportion to its predictability.

Intermediaries in the government context are the career civil service, whose institutional memory, professional norms, and accumulated expertise constitute the actual governance capacity of the agency regardless of who the political appointees are. Political leadership sets priorities; career staff implement, interpret, and in practice often shape those priorities through the discretion inherent in operational decisions.

The diagnostic question for anyone entering political office or a senior agency position — and this is the question Machiavelli would ask — is not what authority the position formally carries but what the career staff will actually do, how fast, and under what conditions. The answer to that question determines what is politically achievable, not the formal authority structure.

Five Questions for Any Institution

The framework elements described above resolve into five questions that can be carried into any institution and applied regardless of its symbolic language. These are not a checklist. They are angles of approach — each one opening a line of inquiry that leads into the institution's actual operating architecture, not its self-description.

1. **Where does this institution's legitimacy actually come from — and what happens when those sources conflict?**

   Every institution claims multiple sources of legitimacy simultaneously. The question is not what claims are made but which source would survive if the others were removed.

   A hospital that claims both medical authority and charitable mission will behave differently in a resource crisis depending on which legitimacy source is load-bearing. A diocese that claims both episcopal authority and pastoral responsiveness will resolve conflicts between them in predictable ways depending on which source the bishop (and the chancery) actually treats as primary.

   Conflict between legitimacy sources is diagnostic: it reveals which the institution is actually organized to protect.

2. **Where does enforcement reliably fall — and what does selective enforcement reveal about actual priorities?**

   Stated values and enforced values diverge in every institution. The question is not what the institution says it values but what violations trigger swift, consistent response and what violations are tolerated, managed quietly, or passed over.

   An academic institution that says it values intellectual diversity but whose social enforcement mechanisms punish only one kind of heterodoxy reveals its actual priority through the pattern of enforcement, not through its mission statement. A government agency that says it enforces its mandate impartially but whose enforcement actions cluster around particular industries, geographies, or political contexts reveals its actual operating priorities in the same way.

3. Who are the actual intermediaries — and where does their discretion shape outcomes more than formal authority does?

The formally powerful and the operationally powerful are often different people. In a parish, the parish administrator and the long-serving deacon may exercise more practical authority over daily institutional life than the pastor. In a university, the registrar and the director of financial aid may shape student experience more concretely than the dean. In a government agency, the senior career staff who managed the program through multiple administrations hold institutional knowledge that political appointees cannot replicate.

The diagnostic question is not who holds the title but whose judgment is deferred to when decisions have to be made quickly, when the rules are ambiguous, and when the formally powerful are absent.

4. What narrative does the institution produce to explain its failures — and what does that narrative protect?

Every institution has a standard explanation for its own failures: individual misconduct instead of systemic design, resource constraints instead of priority choices, external forces instead of internal decisions. These narratives are not necessarily dishonest, but they are structurally self-protective — they locate causation in ways that do not implicate the institution's core operating logic.

The diagnostic question is not whether the explanation offered is entirely false but what it systematically excludes. An institution that always explains failure as the result of bad actors rarely examines the system that selected, promoted, and protected those actors. An institution that always explains failure as resource-constrained rarely examines the priority choices that allocated those resources.

5. What happens to dissent — and what does the treatment of dissent reveal about institutional health?

The treatment of internal dissent is among the most reliable indicators of institutional health available to an observer. Institutions that process dissent — that have real channels through which criticism is heard, considered, and sometimes acted upon — tend to correct errors before they become crises. Institutions that suppress dissent — through retaliation, social exclusion, procedural obstruction, or simple non-response — tend to accumulate errors until they become visible failures.

The diagnostic question is not whether the institution has formal grievance procedures (almost all do) but whether those procedures have ever produced an outcome that cost something to the institution's leadership. Procedures that exist but never produce uncomfortable outcomes are dissent management, not dissent processing.

Institutional literacy produces clarity. It allows the reader to see beyond appearance, beyond moral self-description, and beyond symbolic authority to the operating architecture that governs behavior. Ideals matter within this frame because structures either sustain them or erode them. Moral aspiration without structure dissipates. Structure without legitimacy hardens. Power operates in the space between.

To read institutions clearly is to meet them with steadier attention. It reduces surprise. It increases discernment.

CHAPTER 24

The Effectual Truth and the Examination of Power

If the previous chapter equips the reader to identify institutional mechanisms, this chapter addresses how judgment operates once those mechanisms are visible.

Machiavelli's most enduring provocation is methodological. He insists that political judgment begins from what he called the *effectual truth*: what happens when authority is stressed — when legitimacy fractures, fear enters decision-making, incentives tighten, and necessity compresses the range of choice.[272]

The *effectual truth* shifts attention from intention and proclamation to consequence and structure. It asks how systems behave under pressure and treats power as something exercised within constraints, shaped by incentives, institutions, and the management of risk.

This book has trained that discipline of attention within a particular world: European Christendom, a civilization in which moral language functioned as public infrastructure and institutional continuity often mattered more than personal sanctity. Machiavelli belongs inside that world. He wrote within a political environment saturated with ritual, reputation, law, and coercion, where legitimacy was articulated through moral vocabulary and sustained through institutional practice. His realism reads best as a commitment to political explanation when moral language tempts replacement.

From that vantage point, the task of the reader is clarity: sustained attention to how authority actually operates.

The Thesis at Full Weight

The Introduction announced a mutual-dependency claim: Machiavelli cannot be fully understood without Christendom, and Christendom's institutional mechanics cannot be fully understood without Machiavelli. The reader has now

[272] Machiavelli, *The Prince*, chs. 6–8, 15–18; Skinner, *Foundations*, 130–138.

traveled through the evidence for both halves of that claim. It is worth stating them clearly at the end, with the weight the argument has earned.

What Christendom made possible for Machiavelli is not merely a historical backdrop: it is the epistemic environment that formed his capacity to observe what he observed.

His Latin was ecclesiastical Latin, shaped by a millennium of theological and legal use that gave its key terms — *virtù, fortuna, necessità, gloria* — layers of meaning that his readers would have registered immediately and that he was exploiting deliberately.

His rhetorical formation descended from institutions — cathedral schools, humanist academies operating within Church patronage — that had developed the art of persuasion as a tool of governance and formation.

His political problems were the specific problems of a civilization that had organized itself around competing claims to authority, all of them articulated in Christian moral vocabulary, none of them finally resolved.

There was no vantage point outside this world from which a purely secular political analysis could have been conducted. Machiavelli's analytical power came from being inside the tradition he was diagnosing — understanding its failures with the clarity available only to someone formed by it.

What Machiavelli makes visible about Christendom is the machinery beneath the moral language. Christendom's institutions described themselves in terms of divine order, sacramental legitimacy, and providential purpose. Machiavelli described what they did: how legitimacy was produced and maintained, how enforcement operated when moral consensus fractured, how authority concentrated under necessity, how founding violence was retrospectively justified by what it built, how the gap between institutional aspiration and institutional operation was the permanent condition of political life, not a remediable failure.

His contribution was not to expose Christendom as fraudulent — the institutions were often sincere about their moral claims — but to describe the machinery that operated alongside, beneath, and sometimes in spite of those claims. Without that description, Christendom's institutional legacy is invisible. The university, the corporation, the professional ethics system, the procedural due process that Chapter 20 traced into modernity — these cannot be understood as what they are without understanding the institutional environment that built them and the analyst who described how that environment functioned.

That entanglement extends into modernity. Modern governance is living inside Christendom's institutional inheritance without, for the most part, knowing it. The legitimacy vocabulary has changed — from divine order to rights and dignity, from sacrament to constitution, from vocation to professional identity — but the operating logic has not. Authority still requires justification. Obedience still requires meaning. Conflict still requires channels. Crisis still concentrates decision. Formation still governs behavior more pervasively than enforcement. These are Christendom's problems, Christendom's solutions, operating with secular labels. Understanding this does not require nostalgia for Christendom or skepticism about secular modernity. It requires clarity about what was built, how it works, and what the analyst who first described it clearly was actually doing.

Machiavelli was not launching modernity against the medieval world. He was describing the medieval world's institutional mechanics with a precision that turned out to be portable — because the problems he was describing are the permanent problems of governance, not the temporary problems of one civilization in one period.

Moral and religious formation often encourages an assumption that aspiration implies capacity. Because formation aims at the good, it can slide into the belief that right intention produces effective action. Christendom repeatedly demonstrates the gap. Institutions can sincerely proclaim justice while administering injustice. Leaders can sincerely desire peace while rewarding behaviors that generate conflict. Communities can sincerely revere holiness while elevating ambitions that hollow it out. The pattern follows from misalignment between moral intent and institutional design.

Machiavelli remains useful because he trains a habit of examination. He directs attention to where legitimacy is actually drawn from, where enforcement reliably falls, and how intermediaries translate authority into ordinary life. He attends to reputation, narrative, discipline, and dissent as operating features of durable systems. The resulting questions function diagnostically.

In Christendom, these mechanisms were often visible. Legitimacy drew on divine order, duty, conscience, sacrament, and salvation. Enforcement operated through courts, arms, ecclesiastical discipline, and reputational sanction. Intermediaries filled the landscape: clergy, jurists, administrators, teachers, monastic and guild networks. Narrative coherence was produced publicly through liturgy, preaching, ritual time, shared memory, and Scripture as a common grammar of authority, revolt, fidelity, and failure.

As theological unity fractured, symbolic language changed while operating constraints persisted. Authority required justification. Obedience required meaning. Crisis demanded concentrated decisions. Conflict demanded channels. Institutions re-anchored legitimacy — grace and sin yielding to rights and dignity, sacrament yielding to constitution and expertise — while preserving the functions those categories served. The problems governance must solve remained even as the language used to solve them shifted.

The *effectual truth* functions as a discipline of perception. It trains the reader to recognize that moral language often performs several roles at once: expressing conviction, stabilizing obedience, forming conscience, producing legitimacy, motivating sacrifice, and sustaining institutional continuity. Recognizing this situates moral language within the machinery that allows communities to endure.

That recognition sharpens moral responsibility. Attention to mechanics removes easy refuge. When a leader appeals to good intention, examination turns to outcomes: what the system rewarded, what the structure made likely, and what choices were produced under constraint. When an institution appeals to its ideals, examination turns to practice: where discipline falls, how authority is exercised, and what patterns of character formation reliably emerge. Moral sincerity matters. Consequence completes it.

An Ethical Boundary: Four Points for Those Entering Institutions

The analysis in this book is diagnostic, not prescriptive. It describes how institutions behave; it does not tell readers what to do with what they see. But for readers who expect to operate within institutions in roles that carry authority, responsibility, or strategic influence — whether in government, nonprofits, universities, corporations, media, or religious organizations — a diagnostic framework of this kind has ethical implications that should be stated directly. Four points matter most.

The first is that clarity about institutional mechanics makes moral judgment possible, not impossible. There is a form of idealism that treats clear-eyed analysis of power as a threat to moral commitment — as though seeing how institutions actually work must lead to cynicism, collaboration, or paralysis. The opposite is more often true. Moral judgment without institutional clarity tends toward either naivety or theater: naivety when the leader believes that good intention will carry the day regardless of structural constraints, theater when the leader performs moral commitment in ways that are entirely legible to the institution's incentive structure and therefore entirely absorbed by it without consequence.

A bishop who understands how diocesan administration actually works — which decisions the chancellor makes, how resource allocation signals priority, what enforcement patterns reveal about actual values — is better positioned to reform it than one who governs from a moral altitude above those details. A Jesuit provincial who understands the incentive structure of the institutions he governs is better positioned to shape them than one who relies on the charism doing work that charism alone cannot do. Description supplies the truthful material on which conscience can operate. Without it, conscience is working in the dark.

The second is that moral language can be sincere and structurally operative at the same time — and that this simultaneity is a feature, not a flaw, of institutional life. The Christendom analysis in this book might create the impression that moral language is always or primarily a legitimacy technology: a tool that power uses to make itself palatable. That impression would be wrong, and it would be a misreading of Machiavelli as well. The point is not that moral language is manipulative but that it has institutional effects regardless of whether those effects are intended.

A religious superior who sincerely preaches humility creates institutional conditions in which humility is modeled and rewarded, which shapes the character formation of everyone in the institution — this is the Paul analysis from

Chapter 19 operating at the level of a religious community. The institutional effect is real whether or not the superior intended it. Formation therefore requires attention to outcome as well as intention, not because intention is irrelevant but because outcome is where intention meets the world. Speech about the good shapes systems. That is not a reason to distrust the speech; it is a reason to speak carefully and to watch what happens.

The third is that institutions can do genuine good while exhibiting predictable failure modes, and that the coexistence of good fruit and structural pathology is the normal condition of institutional life, not an anomaly. The Church that built the university and invented procedural due process also conducted the Inquisition and protected abusive clergy. These are not contradictions that cancel each other out; they are the mixed record of a complex institution operating over centuries under the full range of human motivations and institutional incentives. Recognizing this is not cynicism — it is the prerequisite for mature engagement with institutions.

The person who cannot acknowledge the genuine good in an institution they also criticize will not be trusted by those who love it. The person who cannot acknowledge the genuine pathology in an institution they also love will not be useful to those who suffer under it. Mixed outcomes do not cancel the good; they warn against romanticism, which is the most common and most dangerous form of institutional naivety for those entering leadership. Romantic idealization of an institution typically produces either disillusionment — when the reality arrives and cannot be integrated — or complicity, when the person has invested enough of their identity in the institution's self-image that acknowledging its failures becomes existentially threatening.

The fourth is that formation requires a disciplined distinction between aspiration and capacity, and that confusing the two is the characteristic institutional failure of morally serious people. The person who enters an institution with high ideals and confuses those ideals with institutional capacity will be repeatedly surprised by the gap between aspiration and structure. They believe that because the institution aspires to justice it is therefore organized to produce it, because it aspires to pastoral care it is therefore structured to deliver it, because it aspires to truth it is therefore willing to hear it.

When the gap appears, they will typically interpret it as personal failure — their own or others' — rather than as structural condition. Leadership suffers from this confusion because it directs moral energy toward symptoms instead of causes. The institutional reformer who focuses on individuals — on removing bad actors, on finding better leaders, on raising moral standards through exhortation — without attending to the structures that selected, promoted, and protected those actors will find the problems recurring under new names. Moral energy is easily captured by systems it does not understand. Discernment without structural literacy becomes vulnerable to theater — one's own and others' — because theater is exactly what institutions produce to manage moral pressure without changing the incentive structure that generates the problem.

✦

This marks the book's practical endpoint for formation: clarity of register. Moral theology addresses what ought to be. Spiritual theology addresses interior formation and desire. Ecclesiology addresses the Church's nature and mission. This book has worked at a different level: institutional mechanics under constraint. Confusing these registers produces predictable errors — diagnosis mistaken for endorsement, realism mistaken for cynicism, aspiration mistaken for capacity.

Discernment looks steadily at what is happening — externally in structures and internally in motive — without rushing to simplify. It tests moral language against durable practice. It asks where legitimacy comes from, where enforcement falls, who carries authority, and how dissent and reform are handled. It learns to distinguish stability that reflects health from stability produced by silence.

Machiavelli's value at the end of this book lies in training attention at the point where ideals meet necessity and institutions reveal their shape. The reader becomes less easily misled by rhetoric, scandal cycles, moral theater, or the assumption that power operates only where it openly announces itself.

Seeking the Good Inside Institutions You Did Not Design

The reader who has followed this book to its end is likely someone who will spend a significant portion of their life inside institutions — a diocese, a university, an

NGO, a government agency, a religious community, a parish. Some of those institutions they will lead. Many they will inhabit without controlling. All of them will shape what is possible and constrain what the reader can do with the moral commitments they carry into them.

This is the condition Machiavelli describes from beginning to end of his work: the condition of the person who inherits an institutional world they did not design, must act within constraints they did not choose, and is responsible for outcomes that will be shaped by forces they cannot fully control. His answer to this condition is not resignation and not naivety. It is the discipline of clear attention — beginning with what is actually present, what the institution actually rewards, what the constraints actually permit, and what the gap between aspiration and structure actually looks like in this specific place at this specific moment.

That discipline is harder than it sounds, for a particular reason. Institutions have powerful mechanisms for producing in their members a version of institutional reality that protects the institution from clear sight. These mechanisms are not usually conspiratorial — they operate through the normal processes of socialization, reward, professional formation, and the quite human tendency to see the world through the categories of the community one belongs to.

A person who has spent years inside a religious institution will have absorbed that institution's self-understanding, its explanatory vocabulary for its own failures, its account of who its critics are and why they are wrong. That absorption is not weakness; it is the natural result of formation, which is how institutions produce members capable of carrying their purposes forward. But it means that clear sight of one's own institution requires a deliberate effort that clear sight of other institutions does not — and it means that the analytical tools this book has provided are hardest to apply, and most needed, precisely where the reader feels most at home.

The temptation that waits at the end of a book like this is the temptation of analytical detachment — of using institutional literacy as a way of holding every institution at arm's length, of becoming the person who can see clearly because they have declined to invest. That temptation should be named and refused.

Machiavelli was not detached from the institutions he analyzed. He served Florence with genuine commitment. He lost his position, was tortured, and spent years in exile — not because he had maintained safe distance from institutional life but because he had been fully inside it. His analytical clarity was the product of engagement, not its substitute. The effectual truth is not a posture of ironic distance. It is a commitment to seeing what is present precisely because one cares about what happens there.

To seek the good inside institutions you did not design means accepting a specific kind of tension as permanent, not temporary. The tension between what the institution aspires to and what it is currently organized to produce will not resolve. The gap between the moral language used to describe the institution and the mechanics through which it actually operates will not close — not completely, not finally, not in your tenure. This is not a counsel of despair. It is a description of the actual conditions under which institutions are reformed, when they are reformed: through sustained, clear-eyed engagement by people who understand what they are dealing with and continue anyway.

Durable reform in complex institutions has usually come from people who combined moral seriousness with institutional realism in roughly equal measure.

The Gregorian reformers who rebuilt the papacy's administrative apparatus in the eleventh century recognized that the corruption they were confronting was structural, not merely personal, and they built structural responses: canon law, clerical discipline, and institutional accountability.

The conciliarists who confronted the Schism recognized that a constitutional crisis could not be solved by repeating the institution's own self-description, so they advanced a different governing mechanism — the general council — to do what the existing machinery could not.

The Jesuits, for their part, understood that elite formation was itself a form of governance and built one of the most sophisticated training systems in premodern Europe.

None of these reformers were naive about the institutions they inhabited. None stood wholly outside them either. They worked from within, over long time horizons, with clear eyes about the gap between ideals and structures, and treated that gap not as a reason to wait, but as the terrain on which durable change had to be made.

That is the formation this book has aimed at, through a long detour into the political theology of Christendom, the analytical vocabulary of its most penetrating institutional critic, and the specific mechanics through which its institutional legacy arrived in the world the reader inhabits. The detour was necessary because the shortcut — telling the reader to be both idealistic and realistic, both committed and clear-eyed, both inside the institution and able to see it — is not enough. The discipline has to be developed against specific material, in contact with real institutions and their real failure modes, through an analysis that names the mechanisms instead of gesturing at their general existence.

What the reader carries forward is not a method or a checklist or a theory. It is a trained habit of attention: the capacity to ask, in any institutional context, where legitimacy actually comes from, where enforcement reliably falls, who the intermediaries are and what their discretion produces, what narrative the institution tells about itself and what that narrative protects, and what happens to those who dissent. Those questions do not answer themselves. They require the judgment, the moral commitment, and the courage to act on what one sees that no analytical framework can supply. But they make it harder to be fooled — by the institution, by its critics, and by oneself.

✦

If the reader carries anything forward, it should be this: clarity is conscience's precondition in complex systems. Sobriety about power belongs to responsible leadership in a world where authority is always mediated, always constrained, and always capable — through action or neglect — of producing consequences beyond intention.

To seek the good without understanding the machinery that carries it is to risk surrendering that good to forces left unnamed. The *effectual truth* names the machinery and keeps attention there.

EPILOGUE

Reading Power in the Present Tense

The framework assembled across this book is only as useful as what it reveals when aimed at something real. This epilogue applies it to one contemporary institutional crisis — not to deliver a verdict, but to demonstrate what the lens looks like when it makes contact with the present.

The case is the Catholic Church's decades-long governance failure around the sexual abuse of minors by clergy.[273] The abuse itself is a moral catastrophe. This epilogue is not about the abuse. It is about the governance failure — the institutional response, or rather the sustained institutional non-response, that allowed the catastrophe to compound across five decades, multiple continents, and hundreds of thousands of victims.

That failure is chosen deliberately. No other contemporary crisis has produced a documentary record comprehensive enough — grand jury reports, independent diocesan audits, cross-national studies — to make every element of the diagnostic framework visible in public evidence. And when read through that framework, the governance failure is almost entirely predictable.

That is a diagnostic observation, not a comforting one.

Where Legitimacy Came From

The Catholic Church's authority rested, through the period of the abuse crisis, on a legitimacy structure with at least four distinct sources — and the interaction among those sources is the first thing the Machiavellian diagnostic reveals.

Sacramental legitimacy was primary and in some ways impervious. A bishop's authority derived from ordination, not from performance. The office carried weight regardless of how it was exercised — a feature the medieval canonists designed deliberately, for reasons that were institutionally sound in their original

[273] Pennsylvania Grand Jury Report (2018); John Jay College Report (2004).

context, and that had deeply problematic consequences in this one. A bishop who had systematically protected abusive priests was still, canonically, a bishop. His decisions remained valid. His authority remained intact. The separation of office from personal virtue — one of Christendom's great institutional innovations, designed to ensure that the Church could function through weak or sinful occupants — here became a mechanism that insulated the institution from accountability for the conduct of those occupants.

Moral legitimacy sat alongside sacramental legitimacy and in ordinary times reinforced it. The Church's claim to moral authority — to speak credibly on questions of human dignity, sexuality, the protection of children, the obligations of the powerful toward the vulnerable — was real and had been built over centuries of genuine service, genuine institutional achievement, and genuine moral seriousness. That accumulated credibility was the second legitimacy source, and it functioned as a reserve that bishops were drawing down, invisibly, every time they moved an abusive priest instead of removing him. The draw-down was not visible until the reserve was gone.

Institutional loyalty constituted a third legitimacy source, operating primarily among clergy and Catholic laity. The Church was not merely an organization for most of its members; it was the institution within which their identities, communities, and ultimate commitments were organized. That loyalty generated a powerful disposition to accept institutional explanations for troubling events — to credit assurances that the problem was being handled, to extend good faith across a credibility gap that, in any other institutional context, would not have been extended. Institutional loyalty of this kind is not naivety. It is the normal product of deep formation, which is how durable institutions create members capable of sustaining them across generations. Its governance consequence here was a prolonged delay between the accumulation of evidence and the willingness to act on it.

External legitimacy — the Church's standing in civil society, its relationships with political institutions, its capacity to operate schools, hospitals, and social services under favorable regulatory conditions — constituted a fourth source. This source was both a genuine asset and a specific vulnerability: the Church's civil society presence created powerful incentives to avoid the kind of public scandal that would damage it, which reinforced the institutional tendency toward internal management of abuse disclosures rather than external reporting.

Where Enforcement Actually Fell

Here the diagnostic is sharpest. The Church had extensive formal enforcement machinery: canon law, episcopal disciplinary authority, the Congregation for the Doctrine of the Faith, the capacity to defrock priests, remove them from ministry, and impose canonical penalties. What the investigation records — the Pennsylvania grand jury report, the John Jay studies, the independent reviews commissioned diocese by diocese across the United States, Ireland, Germany, Australia, and Chile — show with remarkable consistency is that this enforcement machinery was not deployed against abusive priests. It was deployed, implicitly and sometimes explicitly, against the victims and the people who supported them.

Priests who abused were moved. Families who complained were managed. Dioceses that faced legal exposure settled quietly under confidentiality agreements. Bishops who reported concerns through internal channels found those concerns absorbed without consequence. The pattern is not one of an institution that lacked enforcement capacity. It is one of an institution whose enforcement capacity was organized around a different priority than the stated one: around the protection of institutional reputation and the preservation of clerical culture, rather than around the protection of the children in its care.

This is the *effectual truth* of the governance failure. Not what the Church said it valued — the dignity of every person, the protection of the vulnerable, the pastoral care of those harmed — but what its enforcement patterns actually revealed it was organized to protect. Stated values and enforced values diverged, systematically, over decades, across jurisdictions, under multiple pontificates. That consistency is not the product of individual malice. It is the product of institutional incentive structure — which is exactly what Machiavelli would have looked for first.

The Faction Structure and the Intermediaries

Faction in the clergy sexual abuse crisis did not present itself as faction. It presented itself as a dispute about pastoral approach, about the proper handling of confidential matters, about the relative authority of civil and canon law, about whether publicizing abuse would harm more victims than it helped. These were real questions, and some of the people asking them were asking in good faith. But the faction structure beneath the pastoral vocabulary was simpler: those whose institutional position depended on the existing clerical culture being protected versus those whose institutional position — or whose victims' interest — required it to change.

The intermediaries who determined outcomes were not primarily bishops. They were chancellors, vicars general, canon lawyers, and insurance counsel — the administrative layer that managed disclosures, drafted settlement agreements, arranged reassignments, and maintained the records (or ensured their non-maintenance) that would later become evidence. This is the indirect rule analysis from Chapter 11 applied directly: the bishops set the general orientation, but the operating decisions were made by the administrative apparatus that translated that orientation into specific actions. Many bishops were less architects of the cover-up than beneficiaries of an administrative culture that had already learned what was expected and acted accordingly without needing to be told explicitly.

The dissent channels failed with particular completeness. Priests who reported concerns about colleagues found themselves transferred or marginalized. Lay employees who raised alarms found their employment terminated. Victims who pursued complaints through internal Church processes found those processes designed — not necessarily deliberately, but structurally — to produce outcomes that protected the institution rather than the complainant. The formal grievance machinery existed. It did not process dissent; it managed it. The distinction Chapter 22 drew between dissent processing and dissent management was the institutional reality here.

What the Moral Language Was Doing

The moral language deployed throughout the crisis — by bishops responding to allegations, by diocesan communications staff, by Vatican officials addressing the issue publicly — performed several institutional functions simultaneously, most of which were not the function it appeared to be performing.

Expressions of pastoral concern for victims established a legitimating posture without committing to any specific action. Language about the gravity of the sin and the importance of healing reframed what was a governance failure as a spiritual problem — one whose appropriate response was prayer, repentance, and pastoral care instead of institutional accountability and structural reform. Appeals to the confidentiality of the confessional and the seal of internal Church processes provided a legitimating framework for non-disclosure that was presented as theological obligation, not institutional protection.

None of this required hypocrisy in the ordinary sense. Many bishops who used this language believed it. They were operating within a moral vocabulary that their formation had provided, and that vocabulary was doing what moral vocabulary in institutional contexts always does: organizing the institution's response to pressure in ways that stabilize its authority while appearing to address the underlying problem. This is not a uniquely Catholic failure. It is the failure mode Machiavelli identified for every institution that relies on moral language to do work that institutional reform is the only thing capable of doing.

The moral language became institutionally counterproductive at the moment it was exposed — when the gap between what the Church said and what the Church did became publicly visible and undeniable. At that moment, every subsequent use of the moral language was read through the exposure, and the language that had stabilized authority now accelerated its collapse. This is the reputation analysis from Chapter 10: credibility cannot be restored through symbolic repair when the gap between claim and conduct has been documented at scale. Institutions can often be rebuilt faster than belief.

The Lens and Its Invitation

This diagnostic is not a prosecution. The Catholic Church is not the subject of this epilogue in the way that a defendant is the subject of an indictment. It is the subject in the way that Rome was the subject of Machiavelli's analysis of the republic: as an institution whose governance patterns, read carefully, reveal something general about how institutions work — something that applies beyond this case to every institution that combines genuine moral purpose with the human tendency to protect what has been built.

The Church is also the institution that built the university, invented procedural due process, developed corporate personhood, established the model for professional ethics, and created the most sophisticated formation system in the history of Western civilization. These are not canceled by the governance failure. They are part of the same institutional record — the mixed record that Chapter 23 described as the normal condition of institutions that do genuine good while exhibiting predictable failure modes. The diagnostic does not require choosing between these facts. It requires holding both.

This is what the lens offers. Not cynicism — the view that institutions are always and only self-protective, that moral language is always and only legitimacy technology, that the gap between aspiration and structure is always and only evidence of bad faith. That reading is as naive as the romantic one, in its own way. The lens offers something more demanding: the capacity to hold the genuine good and the genuine failure simultaneously, to ask how each was produced, and to resist the interpretive shortcuts — scandal, hero narratives, institutional defense, institutional prosecution — that substitute for the harder work of understanding how the machinery actually operates.

The argument this book has made — that the analyst and the civilization he diagnosed are entangled at every level, that neither makes full sense without the other — acquires a third term here: the present. Modern institutions — including modern religious institutions — cannot be fully understood without the history that built them, the analyst who first described that history's mechanics clearly, and the trained capacity to read what those mechanics are doing right now, in the institutions the reader actually inhabits.

The reader who has absorbed this book now has a lens. It was ground in the particular conditions of European Christendom. It was sharpened by five centuries of engagement with Niccolò Machiavelli's unsentimental analysis of what those conditions actually produced. It is portable to any institution, in any era, that faces the permanent problems of governance: how to justify authority, sustain obedience, manage conflict, concentrate decision under pressure, and keep the gap between moral aspiration and institutional reality narrow enough that the institution remains credible to those who live inside it.

The invitation is to use it. Not as a weapon, not as a refuge from commitment, but as the precondition for the kind of engagement that might actually change something — the engagement that begins with seeing clearly what is present, naming it without euphemism, and then deciding, with full knowledge of the constraints, what the situation requires.

That is what Machiavelli did, in Florence, in the first decade of the sixteenth century, in the ruins of a republic he had served and lost. He looked at the machinery and described it. The *effectual truth* was his method. It remains available. The present tense is always the hardest place to read power clearly, because the pressure is live and the outcomes are not yet fixed. That difficulty is precisely why the discipline matters most now.

BIBLIOGRAPHY

Aquinas, Thomas. *De Regno.* In *Political Writings,* edited by R. W. Dyson. Cambridge: Cambridge University Press, 2002.

Aquinas, Thomas. *Summa Theologiae.* Translated by Fathers of the English Dominican Province. New York: Benziger Bros., 1947–48.

Arendt, Hannah. *On Violence.* New York: Harcourt, Brace & World, 1970.

Aristotle. *Politics.* Translated by C. D. C. Reeve. Indianapolis: Hackett, 1998.

Augustine. *De civitate Dei.* Translated by Henry Bettenson. London: Penguin, 2003.

Barclay, John M. G. *Paul and the Gift.* Grand Rapids: Eerdmans, 2015.

Beetham, David. *The Legitimation of Power.* Basingstoke: Macmillan, 1991.

Bellah, Robert N. "Civil Religion in America." *Daedalus* 96, no. 1 (1967): 1–21.

Bellomo, Manlio. *The Common Legal Past of Europe.* Washington, DC: Catholic University of America Press, 1995.

Berger, Peter L. *The Sacred Canopy.* Garden City, NY: Doubleday, 1967.

Berlin, Isaiah. "The Originality of Machiavelli." In *Against the Current,* 25–79. New York: Viking, 1979.

Berman, Harold J. *Law and Revolution: The Formation of the Western Legal Tradition.* Cambridge, MA: Harvard University Press, 1983.

Black, Robert. *Humanism and Education in Medieval and Renaissance Italy.* Cambridge: Cambridge University Press, 2001.

Block, Daniel I. *Judges, Ruth.* New American Commentary. Nashville: Broadman & Holman, 1999.

Blumenthal, Uta-Renate. *The Investiture Controversy: Church and Monarchy from the Ninth to the Twelfth Century.* Philadelphia: University of Pennsylvania Press, 1988.

Boase, T. S. R. *Boniface VIII.* London: Constable, 1933.

Boethius. *The Consolation of Philosophy.* Translated by Victor Watts. London: Penguin, 1999.

Boling, Robert G. *Judges.* Anchor Bible 6A. Garden City, NY: Doubleday, 1975.

Bonney, Richard, ed. *The Rise of the Fiscal State in Europe.* Oxford: Oxford University Press, 1999.

Bossy, John. *Christianity in the West 1400–1700.* Oxford: Oxford University Press, 1985.

Boyle, Leonard E., O.P. "The Summa Confessorum of John of Freiburg and the Popularization of the Moral Teaching of St. Thomas." In *St. Thomas Aquinas 1274–1974: Commemorative Studies,* edited by Armand A. Maurer, 245–268. Toronto: Pontifical Institute of Mediaeval Studies, 1974.

Bradford, Sarah. *Cesare Borgia: His Life and Times.* New York: Stein and Day, 1976.

Brown, Peter. *The Rise of Western Christendom.* Oxford: Wiley-Blackwell, 2013.

Brown, Raymond E. *An Introduction to the New Testament.* New York: Doubleday, 1997.

Brucker, Gene A. *The Civic World of Early Renaissance Florence.* Princeton: Princeton University Press, 1977.

Brueggemann, Walter. *First and Second Samuel.* Interpretation. Louisville: Westminster John Knox, 1990.

Brueggemann, Walter. *Theology of the Old Testament.* Minneapolis: Fortress, 1997.

Brundage, James A. *Medieval Canon Law.* London: Longman, 1995.

Casanova, José. *Public Religions in the Modern World.* Chicago: University of Chicago Press, 1994.

Cavanaugh, William T. *Migrations of the Holy.* Grand Rapids: Eerdmans, 2011.

Cavanaugh, William T. *The Myth of Religious Violence.* Oxford: Oxford University Press, 2009.

Chadwick, Henry. *Boethius: The Consolations of Music, Logic, Theology, and Philosophy.* Oxford: Clarendon Press, 1981.

Chastel, André. *The Sack of Rome, 1527.* Translated by Beth Archer. Princeton: Princeton University Press, 1983.

Childs, Brevard S. *Introduction to the Old Testament as Scripture.* Philadelphia: Fortress, 1979.

Clanchy, M. T. *From Memory to Written Record.* 3rd ed. Oxford: Wiley-Blackwell, 2013.

Cobban, Alan B. *The Medieval Universities.* London: Methuen, 1975.

Cohen, Shaye J. D. *From the Maccabees to the Mishnah.* Louisville: Westminster John Knox, 2006.

Colish, Marcia L. *Medieval Foundations of the Western Intellectual Tradition.* New Haven: Yale University Press, 1997.

de Grazia, Sebastian. *Machiavelli in Hell.* Princeton: Princeton University Press, 1989.

Foucault, Michel. *Discipline and Punish: The Birth of the Prison.* Translated by Alan Sheridan. New York: Vintage, 1977.

Fukuyama, Francis. *The Origins of Political Order.* New York: Farrar, Straus and Giroux, 2011.

Gaventa, Beverly Roberts. *When in Romans.* Grand Rapids: Baker Academic, 2016.

Geertz, Clifford. *Local Knowledge.* New York: Basic Books, 1983.

Goldthwaite, Richard A. *The Economy of Renaissance Florence.* Baltimore: Johns Hopkins University Press, 2009.

Gordon, Robert P. *1 & 2 Samuel.* Sheffield: JSOT Press, 1986.

Gorman, Michael J. *Reading Paul.* Eugene, OR: Cascade, 2008.

Gorski, Philip S. *The Disciplinary Revolution: Calvinism and the Rise of the State in Early Modern Europe.* Chicago: University of Chicago Press, 2003.

Gottwald, Norman K. *The Tribes of Yahweh.* Maryknoll, NY: Orbis, 1979.

Grabbe, Lester L. *A History of the Jews and Judaism in the Second Temple Period.* Vol. 2. London: T&T Clark, 2008.

Grafton, Anthony, and Lisa Jardine. *From Humanism to the Humanities: Education and the Liberal Arts in Fifteenth- and Sixteenth-Century Europe.* Cambridge, MA: Harvard University Press, 1986.

Gregory, Brad S. *The Unintended Reformation.* Cambridge, MA: Harvard University Press, 2012.

Grendler, Paul F. *Schooling in Renaissance Italy: Literacy and Learning, 1300–1600.* Baltimore: Johns Hopkins University Press, 1989.

Hamilton, Bernard. *Religion in the Medieval West.* 2nd ed. London: Arnold, 2003.

Hays, Richard B. *The Moral Vision of the New Testament.* New York: HarperCollins, 1996.

Hengel, Martin. *Judaism and Hellenism.* Vol. 1. Philadelphia: Fortress, 1974.

Hirschman, Albert O. *Exit, Voice, and Loyalty.* Cambridge, MA: Harvard University Press, 1970.

Hurtado, Larry W. *Lord Jesus Christ.* Grand Rapids: Eerdmans, 2003.

John Jay College of Criminal Justice. *The Nature and Scope of Sexual Abuse of Minors by Catholic Priests and Deacons in the United States, 1950–2002.* Washington, DC: USCCB, 2004.

Johnson, James Turner. *Just War Tradition and the Restraint of War.* Princeton: Princeton University Press, 1981.

Josephus. *Antiquities of the Jews.* Translated by William Whiston. Various editions.

Kaminsky, Howard. "The Great Schism." In *The New Cambridge Medieval History,* vol. 6, c. 1300–c. 1415, edited by Michael Jones, 674–96. Cambridge: Cambridge University Press, 2000.

Kantorowicz, Ernst H. *The King's Two Bodies: A Study in Medieval Political Theology.* Princeton: Princeton University Press, 1957.

Koselleck, Reinhart. *Futures Past: On the Semantics of Historical Time*. New York: Columbia University Press, 2004.

Kristeller, Paul Oskar. *Renaissance Thought and Its Sources.* Edited by Michael Mooney. New York: Columbia University Press, 1979.

Lemche, Niels Peter. *Early Israel.* Leiden: Brill, 1985.

Lipsky, Michael. *Street-Level Bureaucracy.* New York: Russell Sage Foundation, 1980.

Machiavelli, Niccolò. *Discourses on Livy.* Translated by Harvey C. Mansfield and Nathan Tarcov. Chicago: University of Chicago Press, 1996.

Machiavelli, Niccolò. *Legazioni e commissarie*. Edited by Sergio Bertelli. 3 vols. Milan: Feltrinelli, 1964.

Machiavelli, Niccolò. *The Prince*. Translated by Harvey C. Mansfield. Chicago: University of Chicago Press, 1998.

Maitland, Frederic William. "The Corporation Sole." *Law Quarterly Review* 16 (1900): 335–354.

Mallett, Michael, and Christine Shaw. *The Italian Wars 1494–1559.* Harlow: Pearson Education, 2012.

Mallett, Michael. *Mercenaries and Their Masters: Warfare in Renaissance Italy.* London: Bodley Head, 1974.

Mann, Michael. *The Sources of Social Power.* Vol. 1. Cambridge: Cambridge University Press, 1986.

Mansfield, Harvey C. *Machiavelli's Virtue*. Chicago: University of Chicago Press, 1996.

Markus, R. A. *Saeculum: History and Society in the Theology of St. Augustine*. Cambridge: Cambridge University Press, 1970.

Meeks, Wayne A. *The First Urban Christians.* New Haven: Yale University Press, 1983.

Miller, J. Maxwell. *A History of Ancient Israel and Judah.* Louisville: Westminster John Knox, 1986.

Murphy, James J. *Rhetoric in the Middle Ages: A History of Rhetorical Theory from Saint Augustine to the Renaissance*. Berkeley: University of California Press, 1974.

Najemy, John M. *A History of Florence 1200–1575.* Oxford: Blackwell, 2006.

Najemy, John M. *Italy in the Age of the Renaissance, 1300–1550.* Oxford: Oxford University Press, 2004.

Noth, Martin. *The Deuteronomistic History.* Sheffield: JSOT Press, 1981.

O'Donovan, Oliver. *The Desire of the Nations.* Cambridge: Cambridge University Press, 1996.

O'Malley, John W. *Trent: What Happened at the Council.* Cambridge, MA: Harvard University Press, 2013.

Oakley, Francis. *The Conciliarist Tradition: Constitutionalism in the Catholic Church 1300–1870.* Oxford: Oxford University Press, 2003.

Oakley, Francis. *Natural Law, Laws of Nature, Natural Rights.* New York: Continuum, 2005.

Pennington, Kenneth. *The Prince and the Law.* Berkeley: University of California Press, 1993.

Pennsylvania, Commonwealth of. Fortieth Statewide Investigating Grand Jury. *Report I: Interim—Redacted.* 2018.

Pocock, J. G. A. *The Machiavellian Moment: Florentine Political Thought and the Atlantic Republican Tradition.* Princeton: Princeton University Press, 1975.

Prodi, Paolo. *The Papal Prince: One Body and Two Souls: The Papal Monarchy in Early Modern Europe.* Cambridge: Cambridge University Press, 1987.

Rashdall, Hastings. *The Universities of Europe in the Middle Ages.* 3 vols. Oxford: Clarendon Press, 1895. Rev. ed., 1936.

Reynolds, L. D., and N. G. Wilson. *Scribes and Scholars.* 4th ed. Oxford: Oxford University Press, 2013.

Reynolds, Susan. *Kingdoms and Communities in Western Europe 900–1300.* 2nd ed. Oxford: Clarendon Press, 1997.

Römer, Thomas. *The So-Called Deuteronomistic History.* London: T&T Clark, 2005.

Rubinstein, Nicolai. *The Government of Florence under the Medici (1434–1494).* Oxford: Clarendon Press, 1966.

Schwartz, Daniel R. *2 Maccabees.* Berlin: De Gruyter, 2008.

Shaw, Christine. *Julius II: The Warrior Pope.* Oxford: Blackwell, 1993.

Skinner, Quentin. *The Foundations of Modern Political Thought.* Vol. 1. Cambridge: Cambridge University Press, 1978.

Skinner, Quentin. *Machiavelli: A Very Short Introduction.* Oxford: Oxford University Press, 2000.

Southern, R. W. *Western Society and the Church in the Middle Ages.* Harmondsworth: Penguin, 1970.

Strauss, Leo. *Thoughts on Machiavelli.* Glencoe, IL: Free Press, 1958.

Strayer, Joseph R. *On the Medieval Origins of the Modern State.* Princeton: Princeton University Press, 1970.

Tanner, Norman P., ed. *Decrees of the Ecumenical Councils.* Vol. 1. London: Sheed & Ward, 1990.

Taylor, Charles. *A Secular Age.* Cambridge, MA: Harvard University Press, 2007.

Tentler, Thomas N. *Sin and Confession on the Eve of the Reformation.* Princeton: Princeton University Press, 1977.

Tierney, Brian. *The Crisis of Church and State, 1050–1300.* Toronto: University of Toronto Press, 1988.

Tierney, Brian. *Foundations of the Conciliar Theory.* Cambridge: Cambridge University Press, 1955.

Tierney, Brian. *The Idea of Natural Rights: Studies on Natural Rights, Natural Law, and Church Law, 1150–1625.* Atlanta: Scholars Press, 1997.

Tierney, Brian. *Liberty and Law: The Idea of Permissive Natural Law, 1100–1800.* Washington, DC: Catholic University of America Press, 2014.

Tilly, Charles. *Coercion, Capital, and European States.* Cambridge, MA: Blackwell, 1990.

Tsumura, David Toshio. *The First Book of Samuel.* NICOT. Grand Rapids: Eerdmans, 2007.

Viroli, Maurizio. *Machiavelli.* Oxford: Oxford University Press, 1998.

von Rad, Gerhard. *Old Testament Theology.* Vol. 1. New York: Harper & Row, 1962.

Walzer, Michael. *In God's Shadow: Politics in the Hebrew Bible.* New Haven: Yale University Press, 2012.

Walzer, Michael. *Spheres of Justice.* New York: Basic Books, 1983.

Weber, Max. *Economy and Society.* Edited by Guenther Roth and Claus Wittich. Berkeley: University of California Press, 1978.

Weber, Max. "Politics as a Vocation." In *From Max Weber: Essays in Sociology,* edited by H. H. Gerth and C. Wright Mills, 77–128. New York: Oxford University Press, 1946.

Westbrook, Raymond. *Studies in Biblical and Cuneiform Law.* Paris: Gabalda, 1988.

Wright, N. T. *Paul and the Faithfulness of God.* Minneapolis: Fortress, 2013.

About the Author

Don V Pascal writes on political theology, institutional analysis, and the mechanics of power. His understanding of how ecclesiastical institutions operate — how legitimacy is produced and maintained, how moral language becomes governance infrastructure, how discretion is managed across generations — reflects a familiarity that is not entirely academic in origin.

He writes for people who work inside institutions they can see clearly — and who understand that attention to how power operates is the first condition of responsible action within it, not an alternative to commitment.

Index

A

B

C

D

E

F

G

H

I

J

K

L

M

N

O

P

R

S

T

U

V

www.ingramcontent.com/pod-product-compliance
Lightning Source LLC
LaVergne TN
LVHW010654110826
845149LV00014B/3084

* 9 7 8 1 9 7 1 0 9 3 0 5 5 *